THE JOHN DEWEY LECTURE

The John Dewey Lecture is delivered annually under the sponsorship of the John Dewey Society. The intention of the series is to provide a setting where able thinkers from various sectors of our intellectual life can direct their most searching thought to problems that involve the relation of education to culture. Arrangements for the presentation of the Lecture and its publication by Teachers College Press are under the direction of D. Bob Gowin, Chairperson.

The Dialectic of Freedom

MAXINE GREENE

TEACHERS
COLLEGE
PRESS

Teachers College, Columbia University
New York and London

Published by Teachers College Press, 1234 Amsterdam Avenue,
New York, NY 10027

Library of Congress Cataloging-in-Publication Data

Green, Maxine.
   The dialectic of freedom.

   Includes index.
   1. Education—United States—History.   2. Education—
United States—Philosophy.   3. Liberty.   I. Title.
LA205.G72   1988   370'.973   88-2228

ISBN 0-8077-2898-5
ISBN 0-8077-2897-7 (pbk.)

Manufactured in the United States of America

93 92 91 90 89   2 3 4 5 6

For my Linda

Contents

Foreword

Many dialectics are working in this beautifully written book, and no single formulation will capture the whole. It is a book about social freedom based on naming and resisting and overcoming obstacles in order to achieve freedom. It is a book based on social imagination, speculative audacity, and intimations of power over our futures. Many, many paragraphs are pointed—as a mason points stone-work—with passionate eloquence. It is a good read, and I sincerely invite you to experience the reading of it. I know that no forecasting template of a foreword can substitute for reading.

I welcome this work to the domain of education. We need yeast. We need the heady brew yeast can bring. Maxine asks, "Can we educate for positive freedom?" Like Plato's "Can virtue be taught?" such a question is always relevant. So this book is also a thinker's book, a voyage for the practical cogitator engaging real issues that can be neither solved nor abandoned.

Archie Ammons, the poet, wrote that a poem is a walk. A poem is an event like the events in Archie Ammons's "Corson's Inlet," where fixed categories wash away like sand castles, somehow recombining where the stable and precarious meet. Freedom is a poem. Freedom, like love, is created every day in ways small and demanding, tedious, painful, and endured like time itself. Where the issue is free power over demeaning oppression, the time is always now.

Freedom, like educating, has its resources. Maxine Greene is wonderfully beguiling in leading us across a curriculum of excellence in human thought, feeling, and action. Through this curriculum, we find a complex conceptual map relating to freedom. We find freedom in a dialectic with equality. Both cannot be maximized at the same time, for if every one were equally the same, then the freedom of

diversity would be lost, and if every one were totally free, then some
would gain power over others and equality would be lost. In another
dialectic traceable on this conceptual map, freedom and authority are
connected, because in proper authority positive freedom is achieved.
Likewise freedom of individuality and freedom of a shared world are
in tension. These many dialectics co-exist, run their course, remul-
tiply, and extend. Perhaps for educators, the dialectic between received authority of external knowledge is in tension with the con-
structivist view that human knowledge is a human construction.
The notion of knowledge given antecedently and independently of
knowers, Maxine rejects. In her dialectic, the knower and the known
are co-present, each modifying and shaping the other. This view is
not widespread among scientists socialized into their specific disciplinary matrix, as Thomas Kuhn presents it. Maxine does not write
much about science or mathematics, but it is clear that both can be
read, like language and literature, and can be understood to be
empowering freedoms.

As she writes, we live in a historic period in which much of our
knowledge is a form of technocratic rationality and much of our
direct experience is privatized, consumerist experience. Knowledge
and experience have little to do with each other. The power of
educating to change the meaning of human experience is seldom
found in the public places we call our schools. Until we understand
better than we apparently do just how schooling practices can be
made to be governed by vital conceptualizations of educating, we will
need to pay attention to Greene's call for educating in freedom.
Learning, and learning how to learn, give us freedom from oppression. Meaning, and controlling meaning, is the key to oppression.

Like E. B. White, who wrote that he just wanted to keep the
minutes of his own meeting, we must learn to compose our own
scripts of meaning. We can follow Maxine's example of close reading
of literary arts, history, and philosophy, and respect her great ability
to make public her own meanings. A free society needs freedom of
inquiry in all its institutions and common rooms.

D. Bob Gowin

Introduction

This book arises out of a lifetime's preoccupation with quest, with pursuit. On the one hand, the quest has been deeply personal: that of a woman striving to affirm the feminine as wife, mother, and friend, while reaching, always reaching, beyond the limits imposed by the obligations of a woman's life. On the other hand, it has been in some sense deeply public as well: that of a person struggling to connect the undertaking of education, with which she has been so long involved, to the making and remaking of a public space, a space of dialogue and possibility. All this has meant a continuing effort to attend to many voices, many languages, often ones submerged in cultures of silence or overwhelmed by official declamation, technical talk, media formulations of the so-called "true" and the so-called "real." The aim is to find (or create) an authentic public space, that is, one in which diverse human beings can appear before one another as, to quote Hannah Arendt, "the best they know how to be." Such a space requires the provision of opportunities for the articulation of multiple perspectives in multiple idioms, out of which something common can be brought into being. It requires, as well, a consciousness of the normative as well as the possible: of what *ought* to be, from a moral and ethical point of view, and what is in the making, what *might* be in an always open world.

In contexts of this kind, open contexts where persons attend to one another with interest, regard, and care, there is a place for the appearance of freedom, the achievement of freedom by people in search of themselves. Because these searches have found expression in so many provinces of meaning, I have found it increasingly difficult to limit myself to a single province or a single symbol system. From the beginnings of my career, trying with some difficulty to be accepted as a philosopher of education, I found myself moving back and forth between imaginative literature and philosophy. Troubled by the kinds of positivism that identified existential questions (about birth and death and commitment and anxiety and freedom) with "pseudo-questions," with a domain of meaninglessness, I kept on stubbornly seeking out those questions in fictive and poetic worlds, in personal narratives. Troubled by impersonality, by abstract vantage points, I wanted people to name themselves and tell their stories when they made their statements. I came to believe (or I was taught) that "reality" referred, after all, to interpreted experience. Resisting the notion of a finished, predetermined, objective reality, I became fascinated not merely with multiple modes of interpretation, but with all that fed into interpretation from lived lives and sedimented meanings.

In many ways, this book is an effort to tap what are called the multiple realities of human experience. Yes, it is multidisciplinary; yes, it is an effort to integrate the discursive and the nondiscursive, the propositions of history and philosophy and the articulations of art forms. It seeks an audience of the incomplete and the discontented, those who educate with untapped possibility in mind, with hope for the attainment of freedom in a difficult and resistant world. My hope is to reawaken concern for and belief in a humane framework for the kinds of education required in a technological society. It is to recall those who read to some lost spontaneity, some forgotten hunger for becoming different, becoming new. My hope is to remind people of what it means to be alive among others, to achieve freedom in dialogue with others for the sake of personal fulfillment and the emergence of a democracy dedicated to life and decency.

This book began as a John Dewey Lecture and is presented with a sense of privilege evoked by the association with Dewey's name. Because Dewey himself was so committed to intelligence and freedom, so ill at ease with the routine and the unimaginative, I have no consciousness of being bound to an orthodoxy. The very thought of Dewey and the manner in which he "did" philosophy remain liberating, keep me attuned to open possibility. There is a connection between this openness and the chair in the Foundations of Education, the William F. Russell Chair, I am fortunate to hold at Teachers College. The chair was endowed for the sake of advancing inquiry into the connections between education and freedom, and my various explorations in my various disciplines since being appointed to that chair have all centered around what has become the main theme of this book—and, perhaps, the main theme of my life.

Finally, and without any feeling of subject change or dissonance, this book is dedicated to the remembered life and seeking of a beloved daughter. She was teacher, classicist, musician; she made an art of her short married life; she was a person always reaching for possibility. It was in large measure her radiance that lit my way to whatever completion I have achieved.

The Dialectic of Freedom

CHAPTER 1

Freedom, Education, and Public Spaces

Talk of the free world today is intertwined with talk of economic competitiveness, technology, and power. Talk of personal freedom refers to self-dependence and self-determination; it has little to do with connectedness or being together in community. Americans assume that they were born free. If they can function with any degree of effectiveness, they feel entitled to do as they please, to pursue their fulfillments on their own. To be autonomous and independent: This seems to many to be the American dream. Given the climate of the time, there should be celebrations of that dream coming true. Yet on all sides, official voices speak of irresponsibility, illiteracy, relativism, unethical behavior. The sound of those voices intensifies an uneasiness underlying everyday life, an uneasiness that focuses more and more frequently on education. Is it because of a general inattentiveness in years gone by? An uncertainty with regard to our purposes? An anxiety about what is being communicated to the young, about the culture we are perpetuating in time?

It may be due to a realization of carelessness and, yes, a kind of thoughtlessness. There is a mood not unlike what T. S. Eliot captured in his *Murder in the Cathedral* not very long ago:

> There have been oppression and luxury.
> There have been poverty and licence,
> There has been minor injustice,
> Yet we have gone on living,

> Living and partly living . . .
> We have seen births, deaths and marriages,
> We have had various scandals,
> We have been afflicted with taxes,
> We have had laughter and gossip,
> Several girls have disappeared
> Unaccountably, and some not able to.
> We have all had our private terrors,
> Our particular shadows, our secret fears.
>   (1958, pp. 180–181)

He was rendering what many twentieth-century artists have rendered: a lassitude, a disinterest, an absence of care. Virginia Woolf compared it with being "embedded in a kind of nondescript cotton wool" in contrast to living "consciously" (1976, p. 70). To break with the "cotton wool" of habit, of mere routine, of automatism, is (as we shall see) to seek alternative ways of being, to look for openings. To find such openings is to discover new possibilities—often new ways of achieving freedom in the world.

The "secret fears" afflicting people today may be of sickness, pollution, crime, disorder, nuclear war; and indeed most do go on "living and partly living." A few, here and there, seek technical solutions for what is wrong; but, more often than not, the solutions lack a grounding in significantly shared values and norms. We have only to think of what is proposed to solve the problems presented by homelessness, the AIDS epidemic, teenage pregnancy, drug addiction, suicide. Some people look for comfort in fundamentalist promises and pieties; others seek it among those who think and talk and entertain themselves as they do. There is almost no serious talk of reconstituting a civic order, a community. There are no clearly posed proposals for creating what John Dewey called an "articulate public" (1954, p. 184). There is a general withdrawal from what ought to be public concerns. Messages and announcements fill the air; but there is, because of the withdrawal, a widespread speechlessness, a silence where there might be—where there ought to be—an impassioned and significant dialogue.

We find little evidence of a desire "to think what we are doing" (Arendt, 1958, p. 5), little evidence of thoughtfulness or thought. "Thought," wrote Michel Foucault, "is freedom in relation to what one does, the motion by which one detaches oneself from it, establishes it as an object, and reflects upon it as a problem" (1984, p. 388). He also had consciousness in mind, a moment of being, of mediation between what impinges on one from without and one's response. Lacking such critical perspective, people are not inclined to seek out words. Thought, after all, grows through language; without thought or "freedom in relation to what one does," there is little desire to appear among others and speak in one's own voice. Feeling this way, people are unlikely to search for the spaces where they can come together to establish a "sphere of freedom" (Arendt, 1958, p. 30), involving them in their plurality. They allow themselves to become what Christopher Lasch called "minimal selves" (1984, p. 59), men and women experiencing themselves as overwhelmed by external circumstances, victimized, and powerless. In such circumstances, what difference does it make to see oneself as endowed with freedom or even with "certain inalienable rights"? Does not one have to act upon one's freedom along with others—to take the initiative, to break through some boundary? Does not one have to claim what are called "human rights," to incarnate them in the life of community?

Celebrations of the Constitution and the Bill of Rights continue, but day after day their complex affirmations dwindle into slogans. Very often such slogans are used to justify alien undertakings; they are referred to in connection with so many mean-spirited and violent causes that their normative power seems to have drained away. Stunned by hollow formulas, media-fabricated sentiments, and cost-benefit terminologies, young and old alike find it hard to shape authentic expressions of hopes and ideals. Lacking embeddedness in memories and histories they have made their own, people feel as if they are rootless subjectivities—dandelion pods tossed by the wind. What does it mean to be a citizen of the free world? What does it mean to think forward into a future? To dream? To reach beyond? Few even dare to ponder what is to come.

And yet, those of us committed to education are committed not only to effecting continuities but to preparing the ground for what is to come. With this in mind, I want to explore some other ways of seeing, alternative modes of being in the world; and I want to explore implications for educating at this moment of "reform." My focal interest is in human freedom, in the capacity to surpass the given and look at things as if they could be otherwise. John Dewey sought freedom "in something which comes to be, in a certain kind of growth, in consequences rather than antecedents" (1960, p. 280). We are free, he said, "not because of what we statically are, but in so far as we are becoming different from what we have been." To become different, of course, is not simply to will oneself to change. There is the question of being *able* to accomplish what one chooses to do. It is not only a matter of the capacity to choose; it is a matter of the power to act to attain one's purposes. We shall be concerned with intelligent choosing and, yes, humane choosing, as we shall be with the kinds of conditions necessary for empowering persons to act on what they choose. It is clear enough that choice and action both occur within and by means of ongoing transactions with objective conditions and with other human beings. They occur as well within the matrix of a culture, its prejudgments, and its symbol systems. Whatever is chosen and acted upon must be grounded, at least to a degree, in an awareness of a world lived in common with others, a world that can be to some extent transformed.

A special sort of critical understanding is required, therefore, if persons are not to be overwhelmed by the necessities and determinants that work on every life. Isaiah Berlin has written that we "are enslaved by despots—institutions or beliefs or neuroses—which can be removed only by being analyzed and understood. We are imprisoned by evil spirits which we have ourselves—albeit not consciously—created, and can exorcize them only by becoming conscious and acting appropriately" (1970, p. 143). For Stuart Hampshire, the very notion that we can think of ourselves as thinking beings excludes deterministic explanations of what we do; and he also identifies the human sense of freedom with the "power of reflection and with the self-modifying power of thought" (1975, p. 142). For Dewey, "Social conditions interact with the preferences of an individual—in a way favorable to actualizing freedom only when they develop intelligence, not abstract knowledge and abstract thought, but power of vision and reflection. For these take effect in making preference, desire, and purpose more flexible, alert, and resolute" (1960, p. 287).

People differ, we will discover, when it comes to the promise of rational self-direction (or autonomy or vision) for the gaining of freedom. Marxists link the critical analyses they hope to see with deliberate collective action undertaken to change the world. Neo-Marxists focus on critical consciousness and the kind of self-reflectiveness that will expose the impacts of ideology and mystification on thought. Questions arise as to how we are to counter (in the name of freedom) what Michel Foucault called "power," that which inheres in prevailing discourse, in knowledge itself (1977b, pp. 199–217). Nevertheless, there is general agreement that the search for some kind of critical understanding is an important concomitant of the search for freedom. There is also agreement that freedom ought to be conceived of as an achievement within the concreteness of lived social situations rather than as a primordial or original possession. We might, for the moment, think of it as a distinctive way of orienting the self to the possible, of overcoming the determinate, of transcending or moving beyond in the full awareness that such overcoming can never be complete.

We might think of freedom as an opening of spaces as well as perspectives, with everything depending on the actions we undertake in the course of our quest, the *praxis* we learn to devise. For Jean-Paul Sartre, the project of acting on our freedom involves a rejection of the insufficient or the unendurable, a clarification, an imaging of a better state of things. He wrote of a "flight and a leap ahead, at once a refusal and a realization" (1963, p. 92). There has to be a surpassing of a constraining or deficient "reality," actually perceived as deficient by a person or persons looking from their particular vantage points on the world. Made conscious of lacks, they may move (in their desire to repair them) toward a "field of possibles," what is possible or realizable for them. Few people, quite obviously, can become virtuoso musicians or advanced physicists or world-renowned statesmen, but far more is possible for individuals than is ordinarily recognized. For Sartre, they do not reach out for fulfillment if they do not feel impeded somehow, and if they are not enabled to *name* the obstacles that stand in their way. At once, the very existence of obstacles depends on the desire to reach toward wider spaces for fulfillment, to expand options, to know alternatives. As has been said, a rock is an obstacle only to the one who wants to climb the hill. Not caring, the traveler merely takes another path. He/she is like the gentleman Dostoevsky described in *Notes from Underground* (1864/1961, p. 96), who comes up against a stone wall and simply stops. "For these people a wall is not the challenge that it is for people like you and me who think . . . it is not an excuse to turn back."

The point is not that there are never any excuses; it is that, in classrooms as well as in the open world, accommodations come too easily. It is the case, as Sartre said, that there is an "anguish" linked to action on one's freedom, an anguish due to the recognition of one's own responsibility for what is happening. The person who chooses himself/herself in his/her freedom cannot place the onus on outside forces, on the cause and effect nexus. It is his/her interpretation or reading of the situation that discloses possibility; and yet there is no guarantee that the interpretation is correct. If there is proof to be found, it is only in the action undertaken; and the action itself closes off alternatives. There is always, as in the Robert Frost poem, a "road not taken."

In the chapters to follow, we will see how various human beings (within and outside of imaginative texts) invented life-plans or projects for themselves in the light of readings of their lived worlds, sometimes with the help of others, sometimes (although seldom) alone. We will see women unexpectedly refusing the constrictions of the domestic sphere, oppressed or excluded people reading barriers as surpassable. They were able, as it were, to discover their own freedom in a resisting world; but first they had to perceive it as resistant to desire. "Human reality everywhere," wrote Sartre, "encounters resistances and obstacles which it has not created, but these resistances and obstacles have meaning only in and through the free choice which human reality is" (1956, p. 599). The wall has to be viewed as a personal challenge, as an obstacle; but it becomes such only to those risking free choice.

Dewey also saw the relation between freedom and experienced resistance. He, too, believed that people do not think about or go in search of freedom "unless they run during action against conditions that resist their original impulses. . . ." He did not go on to define freedom as the release of all such "original impulses" or to conceive education as an affair primarily of impulse. His concern, as we have seen, was to encourage free and informed choosing within a social context where ideas could be developed "in the open air of public discussion and communication" (1960, p. 286). The resistances that required naming included limitations on free speech, mindlessness, mechanism, routine behaviors, the rule of "brute" habit—none of which would be noticed by those who were somnolent or who had no wish to move beyond. At once, conditions were to be created that allowed for the release of spontaneous preferences, social conditions that might empower persons to act, to become different, to grow. This, in turn, would happen only if persons were enabled to test their own capacities, to use their minds. And, as Dewey wrote, "mind" should be thought of as primarily a verb. "It denotes all the ways in which we deal consciously and expressly with the situations in which we find ourselves" (1934, p. 263). He, too, was concerned about attentiveness to the actualities of life, about the need for all sorts of persons to learn to read their own lived worlds. Clearly this relates to the kind of critical interpretation that gives content to the idea of freedom, that reveals lacks and deficiencies, and that may open the way to surpassing and repair.

The language of contemporary schooling and, indeed, of proposed reforms emphasizes something quite different from such interpretive thinking. Rather than being challenged to attend to the actualities of their lived lives, students are urged to attend to what is "given" in the outside world—whether in the form of "high technology" or the information presumably required for what is called "cultural literacy." There is, in consequence, an implicit encouragement of the tendency to accede to the given, to view what exists around us as an objective "reality," impervious to individual interpretation. Finding it difficult to stand forth from what is officially (or by means of media) defined as real, unable to perceive themselves in interpretive relation to it, the young (like their elders) are all too likely to remain immersed in the taken-for-granted and the everyday. For many, this means an unreflective consumerism; for others, it means a preoccupation with *having* more rather than *being* more. If freedom comes to mind, it is ordinarily associated with an individualist stance: It signifies a self-dependence rather than relationship; self-regarding and self-regulated behavior rather than involvement with others. Above all, it means an absence of interference or (to use the idiom of the federal government) a deregulation. People consider themselves free if the road is opened before them—to pursue success or security or status, to "get ahead." Others are more likely to think in terms of expressivism, of satisfying desire, of giving impulse free play. On occasion, the two notions are linked: One pursues success; one achieves so that one can indulge oneself. But there are still those who believe that nothing really matters in the long run, risk or no risk, except the play of spontaneous energies and the fulfillment (perhaps momentary) of desires.

Charles Taylor has written that the "self which has arrived at freedom by setting aside all external obstacles and impingements is characterless, and hence without defined purpose" (1985, p. 157). There is a danger of nihilism, he thinks, associated with a view of freedom as pure autonomy or self-dependence. There is an equivalent danger in the idea of freedom as an indulgence of the instinctual and the irrational—a danger we see before us every day. Taylor is concerned about finding a conception of what he calls "situated freedom," a conception of free activity seen "as a response called for by a situation which is ours in virtue of our condition as natural and social beings, or in virtue of some inescapable vocation or purpose. What is common to all the varied notions of situated freedom is that they see free activity as grounded in the acceptance of our defining situation. The struggle to be free—against limitations, oppression, distortions of inner and outer origin—is powered by an affirmation of this defining situation as ours" (p. 160). Not only does he empha-

size the fact that we, and our situations, are both natural *and* social;
he relates the notion of "inescapable vocation or purpose" to the idea
of freedom. It is difficult not to be reminded of Paulo Freire writing
of "humanization" as our primary vocation—the struggle for "the
overcoming of alienation," for the affirmation of men and women as
persons (1970, p. 28). It is a matter of affirming human beings as
"subjects of decisions" rather than objects, of involving men and
women in the striving toward their own "completion"—a striving
that can never end.

It is with a similar concern for the human vocation and for
situatedness that I speak of the "dialectic of freedom" in the chapters
of this book. I am eager to reaffirm the significance of desire along
with the significance of thought and understanding; I want to break
through, whenever possible, the persisting either/ors. There is, after
all, a dialectical relation marking every human situation: the relation
between subject and object, individual and environment, self and
society, outsider and community, living consciousness and phenome-
nal world. This relation exists between two different, apparently
opposite poles; but it presupposes a mediation between them. Take,
for example, the relation between the living subject—a person with
the capacity for reflection, for choosing, for moving beyond himself/
herself—and the object, be it artifact or natural organism or construction. The person comes in touch with the object—let us say, a
table—by means of experience or by grasping it through an act of
consciousness. Its function is clear to the extent that the person
recognizes the table and sees some resemblance between it and
tables known and used in the biographical past. One might say that
the "reality" of the table actually emerges in the course of the
encounter with it; it refers to the person's interpreted experience
with that table and with other tables, as it is thematized and symbol-
ized by language, by its name. This is what is suggested by the
notion of mediation, something that occurs between nature and
culture, work and action, technologies and human minds. Always,
there is a type of tension; but it is not the type of tension that can be
overcome by a triumph of subjectivity or objectivity. Nor is it the
kind of dialectic that can finally be resolved in some perfect synthesis
or harmony. "In thought as in life," wrote Maurice Merleau-Ponty,
"the only surpassings we know are concrete, partial, encumbered
with survivals, saddled with deficits" (1968, p. 99). The effects of
early experience survive, along with the sedimentations of meaning
left by encounters with a changing world. There are the effects of
environment, class membership, economic status, physical limita-

tions, as well as the impacts of exclusion and ideology. The growing, changing individual (no matter how reflective and autonomous he/she appears to be) always has to confront a certain weight in lived situations, if only the weight of memory and the past. There are ambiguities of various kinds, layers of determinateness. Freedom, like autonomy, is in many ways dependent on understanding these ambiguities, developing a kind of critical distance with respect to them. Even when understood, however, even when analyzed, they still exist as factors (more or less repressed) in a human career.

Freedom can be attained through the refusals and realizations of which Sartre spoke, through the kinds of action and dialogue Dewey had in mind. But the freedom achieved can only involve a partial surpassing of determinateness: the limits, internal and external, experienced by restless, preoccupied, rebellious women; the neglect and indifference suffered by the outsider or the immigrant; the discrimination and inequitable circumstances faced by the minority group member; the artificial barriers erected in the way of children trying to create authentic selves. None of these can be considered unreal or merely imagined. All have, as has been said before, to be perceived as obstacles, most often obstacles erected by other human beings (sometimes, but not always, in complicity with the self involved), if freedom is to be achieved. These obstacles or blocks or impediments are, as it were, artifacts, human creations, not "natural" or objectively existent necessities. When oppression or exploitation or segregation or neglect is perceived as "natural" or a "given," there is little stirring in the name of freedom, at least as freedom will be explored in this text. When people cannot name alternatives, imagine a better state of things, share with others a project of change, they are likely to remain anchored or submerged, even as they proudly assert their autonomy. The same, paradoxically or not, is true when people uproot themselves, when they abandon families, take to the road, become strangers in desperate efforts to break loose from pre-established orders and controls.

In both cases—submerged or free-floating—a situated freedom has been abandoned. The Czech novelist, Milan Kundera, has rendered this paradox in *The Unbearable Lightness of Being* (1984). The phrase of the title refers most directly to the condition of being an émigré, rootless, even nameless, never knowing what one wants— "the sketch that is our life a sketch for nothing, an outline with no picture." This is because, having left one's home place, one becomes situationless—intentionally or not (like thousands upon thousands of newcomers in this country today). The artist Sabina leaves her native land in Kundera's novel, and she wanders around America, which she likes. "But only on the surface. Everything beneath the surface was alien to her. Down below, there was no grandpa or uncle. She was afraid of shutting herself into a grave and sinking into the American earth. And so one day she composed a will in which she requested that her dead body be cremated and its ashes thrown to the winds. . . . She wanted to die under the sign of lightness. She would be lighter than air." She is free; but her freedom is a void.

In Kundera's context, the "lightness" is usually opposed to the weight of felt fatality, to determinism, to the pressure of "kitsch." He associates "kitsch" with brass bands and parades, with high-flying abstractions, with old-time pieties. The vocabulary of American kitsch is made up of phrases like "our traditional values," "the barbarity of Communism," and so on. The European kitsch has often to do with the "Grand March" or "the splendid march on the road to brotherhood, equality, justice, happiness; it goes on and on, obstacles notwithstanding, for obstacles there must be if the march is to be the Grand March. The dictatorship of the proletariat or democracy? Rejection of the consumer society or demands for increased productivity? The guillotine or an end to the death penalty? It is all beside the point. What makes a leftist a leftist is not this or that theory but his ability to integrate any theory into the kitsch called the Grand March." For the author, kitsch is integral to the human condition. Its true function is to serve as a folding screen set up to curtain off death, or to mystify by putting a smiling face on things. It is not enough, however, to recognize it as an illusion or a lie, if the achievement of freedom is our concern. It might lose its authoritarian power, but we might be left in the "lightness of being," with our figurative ashes blowing in the wind.

Our theme, again, has to do with the dialectic—in this case, most likely, the dialectic between the "lightness" of the émigré, wandering life and the determinism of the endless March or what the author calls *es muss sein*. In the novel, someone finds a "field of unexpected freedom" in his battle against the *es muss sein* "rooted deep inside him . . . planted there not by chance . . . by anything external." He gives up surgery for window-washing, love for erotic activities, life for death. We will take note of American figures of that sort, in search of negative freedom, of escape or release. We can recall individuals like Daniel Boone, who could not stay in one place, taking off for the woods or the frontier; we can recall the thousands who went off to sea to escape domestic life; we can recall the expatriates who left their home towns for the European cities; we can think of the "hippies" heading for Haight-Ashbury in the heady days of the 1960s, when "liberation" was the watchword and songs were sung about "leaving home" just for the sake of leaving and for getting parents "out of the way." At once, we can remember the numerous victims of small-town provincialism (as in Sherwood Anderson's *Winesburg, Ohio*), of frontier and strikebreaking violence, of back-country isolation, of the underside of the American wilderness—the native *es muss sein*. There have been as many tales of submergence as there have been of emergence and emancipation in our tradition; and the unanswered questions regarding situated freedom remain.

There are a few more clues to be found now, oddly enough in the work of another Czech novelist, Josef Skvorecky, especially in his novel, *The Engineer of Human Souls* (1984), with its chapters headed "Poe," "Hawthorne," "Twain," "Crane," "Fitzgerald." The narrator here recalls being an adolescent in Nazi-occupied Czechoslovakia. He thinks that freedom may be "purely a matter of youth and dictatorships. That it exists nowhere else, perhaps because we are not aware of it. Just as we are unaware of air until, in the gas chamber of life, it is replaced by those crystals, tasteless, colourless, odourless." I think he means that there is no consciousness of obstruction, no resentment or restraint, when a person experiences no desire to change or to question, like (we must all suppose) so many people now living under dictatorships. If there is nothing a person particularly wants to say, he/she will not suffer from censorship or controls on freedom of speech. The individual simply feels free: It is no different than breathing; the condition simply *is*.

Under dictatorships, the ones who have an awareness of freedom are those who do have something they want to say that they are not allowed to say. Desiring to speak and write their own words, they experience the controls of the dictatorship as concrete barriers to their very beings. They take the obstruction personally; it is the way in which their lived situations speak to them. To be something other than an object, a cipher, a thing, such a person must reach out to create an opening; he/she must engage directly with what stands against him/her, no matter what the risk. Because existing dictatorships bear down so heavily on individuals who refuse to comply, they cannot but feel the air replaced by "those crystals, tasteless, colourless" that choke people to death. And so they fight for air. That is probably why the most potent affirmations with respect to freedom and human rights are to be found in writings coming out of eastern Europe. It may be why certain Americans resonate to such a degree to the language and poetry of Solidarity in Poland, to the underground songs in the Soviet Union, to the demonstrations in Chile, to the schoolchildren's protests in South Africa. They are resonating to individuals working and fighting in collaboration with one another, discovering together a power to act on what they are choosing themselves to be.

All this holds relevance for a conception of education in what is described as our free society. It is through and by means of education, many of us believe, that individuals can be provoked to reach beyond themselves in their intersubjective space. It is through and by means of education that they may become empowered to think about what they are doing, to become mindful, to share meanings, to conceptualize, to make varied sense of their lived worlds. It is through education that preferences may be released, languages learned, intelligences developed, perspectives opened, possibilities disclosed. I do not need to say again how seldom this occurs today in our technicized, privatized, consumerist time. The dominant watchwords remain "effectiveness," "proficiency," "efficiency," and an ill-defined, one-dimensional "excellence." Reforms or no, teachers are asked to teach to the end of "economic competitiveness" for the nation. They are expected to process the young (seen as "human resources") to perform acceptably on some level of an increasingly systematized world. Of course, exceptions are made for the privileged and talented, for whom multiple and diverse literacies are made available; but, except in cases of hopeless neglect, the major focus is and will be on technical or "coping" skills. Whether the students are rich or poor, privileged or deprived, the orientation has been to accommodation, to fitting into existing social and economic structures, to what is given, to what is inescapably *there*.

Little, if anything, is done to render problematic a reality that includes homelessness, hunger, pollution, crime, censorship, arms build-ups, and threats of war, even as it includes the amassing of fortunes, consumer goods of unprecedented appeal, world travel opportunities, and the flickering faces of the "rich and famous" on all sides. Little is done to counter media manipulation of the young into credulous and ardent consumers—of sensation, violence, criminality, things. They are instructed daily, and with few exceptions, that human worth depends on the possession of commodities, community status, a flippant way of talking, good looks. What they are made to believe to be the "news" is half entertainment, half pretenses at being "windows on the world." They witness political realities played out in semi-theatrical or cinematic terms. They watch candidates being marketed and withdrawn. In the midst of the marketing and the sounds of sitcom shotguns, there are opportunities to become *voyeurs* of starvation, massacres, torture. And the beat of MTV goes on and on.

In the face of all this, school people are asked to increase academic rigor, ensure the preparation of a work force for "high technology," enhance cultural literacy, overcome mediocrity, contain adolescent pregnancies, prevent suicides, educate against AIDS. Confronting some of the most tragic lacks in American society, some of the saddest instances of dehumanization, they offer promises of "career ladders," "board certification," decision-making power, talk resembling what Kundera calls "kitsch." At once, teachers and administrators are helped still to see themselves as functionaries in an instrumental system geared to turning out products, some (but not all) of which will meet standards of quality control. They still find schools infused with a management orientation, acceding to market measures; and they (seeing no alternatives) are wont to narrow and technicize the area of their concerns.

The person who might indeed find relevant to his/her sense of vocation the dehumanizing forces in the society is not asked to notice them and perceive them as obstacles to becoming. Nor is much done to empower students to create spaces of dialogue in their classrooms, spaces where they can take initiatives and uncover humanizing possibilities. The crisis implicit in what Dewey called the erosion or the "eclipse" of the public is generally ignored. Explorations in the domains of the arts are seldom allowed to disrupt or defamiliarize what is taken for granted as "natural" and "normal." Instead, the arts are either linked entirely to the life of the senses or the emotions, or they are subsumed under rubrics like "literacy."

We are seldom privy to discussions about the education of free men and women in these times, or about the plight of newcomers, especially those who—in their pluralities—are entering into the schools. It has been said that this may be a reaction to the extravagant claims made for the public schools in years past. It is also conceivable that policy-makers are deliberately or incidentally making the school system into what Marcus Raskin once called a "channeling colony" (1971, pp. 342 ff.) geared to training instruments for the state. Whether or not the schools are as intentionally controlling and hegemonic as radical critics have said they are, the constant bombardment of official proposals has led to a preoccupation with preparing the young for a society that will no longer be an industrial one, but rather one committed to "high technology." Little attention is paid to the argument that poorly paid "third world" workers will do assembly line work and can be expected (given the dictatorships they work under) to continue doing so. Little attention is paid to the de-skilling that may take place on a wide scale, as technology develops further; few, if any, proactive questions are posed as to the kind of technologies that might make the workplace more challenging and humane. Emphasis on skills, on proficiencies, on achievements, on techniques responds necessarily to the ambitions and anxieties of parents, including immigrant parents. If the young are to "make it," to "get ahead," if they are to have any options other than retail stores or lunch counters, the schools must demonstrate their effectiveness by equipping students of all groups to meet current market demand.

Even those teachers whose projects have been otherwise are constrained by state action plans and testing mechanisms. The rebellious teacher, the "reflective practitioner" (Schon, 1983) is asked to tamp down dissonant conceptions of what education might be and perhaps ought to be in a chaotic, uncertain time. We do not know how many educators see present demands and prescriptions as obstacles to their own development, or how many find it difficult to breathe. There may be thousands who, in the absence of support systems, have elected to be silent. Thousands of others (sometimes without explanation) are leaving the schools. Surpassing, transcendence, freedom: Such notions are not being articulated in the conversations now going on. And yet, as will be argued in this book, a teacher in search of his/her own freedom may be the only kind of teacher who can arouse young persons to go in search of their own. It will be argued as well that children who have been provoked to reach beyond themselves, to wonder, to imagine, to pose their own questions are the ones most likely to learn to learn.

The fable called "The Grand Inquisitor" in Dostoevsky's *The Brothers Karamazov* (1879–80/1945, p. 292 ff.) comes insistently to mind. The issue there is the tension between what the Inquisitor calls "the promise of freedom which men in their simplicity and their natural unruliness cannot even understand, which they fear and dread" and the guarantee of bread, peace of mind, and happiness to those who acquiesce. Human beings, he says, do not have the strength to tolerate the "vague and enigmatic"; they want something they can all believe in together; they want a shared certainty. In a peculiar fashion, the promise implicit in the proposals of a government that withholds support, that stresses individual responsibility, is a promise of wealth, security, and happiness. Below the surfaces there is a whispered reminder that, if an individual plays the game, smiles, and works hard, he/she will be rewarded. The Inquisitor says that those who rebel and are proud of their rebellion are merely children "rioting and barring out the teacher at school." He says that they will eventually see "the foolish children, that, though they are rebels, they are impotent rebels, unable to keep up their own rebellion." There is little need for security police to keep order if enough people internalize this view, if they perceive themselves as passive audiences and accept that role, if they convince themselves that they are powerless in the face of the tragicomedy being enacted (even if, somehow or other, they expect it all to end in AIDS or in planetary death).

It is difficult to posit obstacles in such an interpreted world. Ordinary life provides distractions and comforts for those who might be expected to go in search. They live among representations, images, symbolic renderings of what might seem (if it were felt and smelled) "the gas chamber of life." In schools, like other institutions, there are memos, not actual barriers to reflective practice. There are conference and commission reports, not barbed wire fences in the way. There are assured, helpful, bureaucratic faces, not glowering antagonists to growth and freedom and an enlarged sense of being in the world. The "weight" is only dimly felt; yet, for many it is accepted as what Milan Kundera describes: It *must* be; *es muss sein.*

We might recall now and then the many instances of human action against what appeared to be similarly vague and similarly unalterable. Hannah Arendt has described the poet René Char's recollections of belonging to the French Resistance during the Second World War (1961, pp. 3–5). He spoke of the ways in which the members of his group came together without masks or pretenses or badges of office, how they felt they had been visited for the first time in their lives by an "apparition of freedom." It was not because they were taking action against tyranny (since armies of men were doing that as well) "but because they had become 'challengers,' had taken the initiative upon themselves and therefore, without knowing or even noticing it, had begun to create that public space between themselves where freedom could appear." They had, as it were, posited what the Nazis were doing in France as obstacles to their own projects, affronts to their own chosen principles, barriers to their self-realization. Although there was no guarantee that the occupation of France would end in their lifetimes, they refused to assume that conditions were unchangeable. By *naming* the atrocities and the repression as obstacles to their shared existential undertakings, they focused attention on them as factors to be resisted, to be fought, perhaps to be overcome. Jean-Paul Sartre noted that such people acted upon what they chose as their responsibility. They were not compelled to do so; but they chose "to live" the war. They could have treated the occupation as a four-year vacation, a reprieve, or a recess; they could have retreated from it with the claim that their major responsibilities lay with their families or their professions. Instead, they came together to reject a state of things they had decided was intolerable. They would not have felt it to be intolerable if they had no possibility of transformation in mind, if they had been unable to imagine a better state of things. Again, it is partly a matter of being able to envisage things as if they could be otherwise, or of positing alternatives to mere passivity. And it should remind us of the relation between freedom and the consciousness of possibility, between freedom and the imagination—the ability to make present what is absent, to summon up a condition that is not yet.

I bring up the case of the Resistance not because the situation we are living through resembles the situation in wartime France. Nor do I bring it up because I believe that extreme situations have to be created if freedom is to be achieved. What appears most deeply relevant is the idea of the Resistance fighters taking the initiative "among themselves" in a shared effort to test the limits, to try to bring about change. They were ostensibly free French citizens before the war; they might simply have complained that their antecedent rights and liberties were being infringed. They could have referred, in other words, to what has been called "negative freedom," the right not to be interfered with or coerced or compelled to do what they did not choose to do. If they had, they might well have spoken of themselves as rational human beings entitled to have their integrity and independence acknowledged. They might have made the point that to be rational is to be capable of self-direction, and that the very capability makes a claim on others, a moral claim that is not to be denied.

Granting the impossibility of making a moral claim under the conditions of Nazi occupation, it is interesting to note that these people (according to Char) believed that the "apparition of freedom" was visiting them for the first time in their lives. Not only does this suggest that they did not view freedom as a gift or an endowment; they did not *feel* free in some interior dimension of their beings. It suggests that freedom shows itself or comes into being when individuals come together in a particular way, when they are authentically present to one another (without masks, pretenses, badges of office), when they have a project they can mutually pursue. When people lack attachments, when there is no possibility of coming together in a plurality or a community, when they have not tapped their imaginations, they may think of *breaking* free, but they will be unlikely to think of breaking through the structures of their world and creating something new. It does not matter whether those structures are as everyday as constraining family rituals, as banal as bureaucratic supervisory systems, as shabby as segregation practices. There must be a coming together of those who choose themselves as affected and involved. There must be an opening of a space between them, what Hannah Arendt called an "in-between" (1958, p. 182), deeper and more significant than merely practical or worldly interests.

When we contrast such a view with the various ways in which freedom is today conceived, we may be enabled to understand why there are so few "challengers" in the United States today. Also, we may be able to discover why so little is done in schools and colleges to empower young people to seek out openings in their lived situations, to tolerate disruptions of the taken-for-granted, to try consciously to become different than they are. It is not a question of freedom being neglected as an official value in America, a kind of icon. For all the absence of dialogue about what it signifies to educate free men and women in these times, there is a constant emphasis on free choice and self-reliance, on people overcoming dependency and taking responsibility for themselves. The official rendering derives from the late eighteenth and early nineteenth centuries, from (it must be recalled) the early days of capitalism. The themes derive from an early liberalism associated with *laissez-faire* approaches to the economy. Deregulation, noninterference, privatization: All are linked to the development of "character," to consumption, to merit, to (deserved) material gain. The support systems once devised to sustain the disadvantaged and the sick have been chipped away; and the arguments have often been libertarian. To be left to one's own devices, to rely on one's own powers is to become stronger, more vital, more effective, or so it is said. Civil rights legislation and affirmative action arrangements are treated as infringements on people's liberties; social programs are considered not only "wasteful" but injurious to "character." Public servants seldom acknowledge any longer what was once considered a "right" to income support when needed, or to housing, or to medical attention. And, quite obviously, the wealthy, the advantaged, benefit from this new attention to freedom.

John Dewey made that point almost half a century ago. When obstructions are removed in the economic domain, the "robber barons," the bankers, the financiers always have benefited. "But," wrote Dewey, "it left all the others at the mercy of the new social conditions brought about by the freed powers of those advantageously situated. The notion that men are equally free to act if only the same legal arrangements apply equally to all—irrespective of differences in education, in command of capital, and the control of the social environment which is furnished by the institution of property—is a pure absurdity" (1960, p. 271). If freedom is considered to be an endowment or a kind of inheritance or a possession to be released by the removal of constraints, its expression cannot but be a function of randomly distributed strengths and capacities. Isaiah Berlin has written that "to offer political rights, or safeguards against intervention by the state to men who are half-naked, illiterate, underfed, and diseased is to mock their condition; they need medical help or education before they can understand, or make use of, an increase in their freedom." Then he went on to make the point that the minimum freedom the poor peasant needs today and the greater degree of freedom he may need tomorrow "is not some species of freedom peculiar to him, but identical with that of professors, artists, and millionaires" (1970, p. 122).

Crucial is the recognition that conditions must be deliberately created to enable the mass of people to act on their power to choose. But they must not be created with the attitude of "pity" that made the Grand Inquisitor distance people, infantilize them, and link the desire for "bread" inextricably with the desire for certainty, for a comfortable mindlessness. Hannah Arendt has written that the Grand Inquisitor's sin was that he depersonalized the sufferers, "lumped them into an aggregate—the people *toujours malheureux*" (1963, p. 80). The antithesis of such an attitude is that characterized by compassion, which is directed toward human beings in their singularity. In our exploration of freedom, we are going to identify life stories of men and women who achieved their freedom in compassion for others or in solidarity with others. They did not exclude or leave others to their own devices; they did not make them objects of charity or pity; they did not deprive persons (as Isaiah Berlin put it) of what they themselves "found indispensable to their life as unpredictably self-transforming human beings."

This may be what we lack today in classrooms and in society as a whole. On the one hand, we are bombarded with talk of self-sufficiency, of what is paradoxically called "choice." On the other, we are confronted with vague talk of rights and entitlements, of a "welfare state" that will satisfy the needs now ignored but may well create what Michael Ignatieff calls "a society of strangers"—a society where material needs are satisfied, but where the needs for consolation, solidarity, love remain unmet (1984). There are strangers all about us now, presumably autonomous people moving in the shopping malls, up the elevators in glass and metal buildings, through antiseptic corridors, in large and muffled rooms. There are masses of strangers on the main streets; but the cities are marked in many places by the emptiness and silences seen in Edward Hopper's paintings. Suburbs and small towns are deserted in the daylight; at night, the walls close people in; and, everywhere, television screens glimmer and speechless onlookers gaze. Richard Sennett writes: "Intimate vision is induced in proportion as the public domain is abandoned as empty. On the most physical level, the environment prompts people to think of the public domain as meaningless" (1979, p. 41). There are few places where individuals are impelled to come together in speech and action, few arenas where (as René Char put it) freedom can "sit down."

Of course, most Americans are convinced they are free: They are not held hostage; they are not enslaved; they are seldom pursued. They do come together, of course, in echoing churches, at rock concerts, in baseball stadiums, in movie theatres. Millions are linked by the same soap operas, quiz shows, talk shows, advertisements for consumer goods. They know by now that they can have babies out of wedlock, take to the roads, sample cocaine, run as long and as far as they please. If adult, they can read what they like—from pornography to romance tales, from exposés of the CIA to revelations about celebrities, from Zen philosophy to probes of artificial intelligence, from modern formalist novels to picture books. Laws or no laws, many feel free to carry guns and knives, to cheat, to sell inside information. Even so, many are likely to share a feeling of subservience to a system, or to a faith, or to an Establishment they can scarcely name.

In *Habits of the Heart*, Robert Bellah and his associates say that freedom is the most deeply held value in this country, yet it "turns out to mean being left alone by others, not having other people's values, ideas, or styles of life forced upon one, being free of arbitrary authority to work, family, and political life." They suggest, however, that Americans find it very difficult to define what they might do with their freedom. It leaves them, too, "with a stubborn fear of acknowledging structures of power and interdependence in a technologically complex society dominated by giant corporations and an increasingly powerful state" (1985, p. 23). This means (according to what has already been said) that they find it difficult to *name* the obstacles in their way. If they are afraid of acknowledging structures, they can scarcely think of breaking through them to create others, to transform.

We are familiar with those who move through them in search of status, who identify their freedom with their striving for success. There are others, in the middle class particularly, who are alienated by technical talk and role-playing, and who go in search of some "intimate terrain" where they hope to discover what they think of as their "real selves." Such discoveries are often associated with "liberation," a state in which inner realities are thought to remain inviolate while ordinary life is lived in the commonsense world. Such people build private shelters, as it were, in which to take refuge from "outer" ambiguities. They attend to what Sartre called a "mysterious psychism" they locate at the center of their beings, something intangible and original, protected against tampering and controls. This permits them to function as they are expected to do where work is done and the system's requirements are fulfilled. They manage to separate, as Dewey put it, "the inner from the outer," to distance themselves from their own social realities. Once distanced, protected against others' judgments and purposes, they feel themselves to be relatively untrammelled and sometimes dangerously "free." They can afford outward compliance, so they tolerate and sometimes become complicitous with what they condemn. Within themselves, they manage to believe, they are pure as well as free.

There are echoes of an old romanticism in this attitude, of old rebellions against mechanisms, schedules, clocks, crowds. It frequently involves, however, misconceptions of what consciousness means, and mind and self as well. And these misconceptions lead many people to identify personal liberation with an abandonment of social involvement and concern. Cynical about reform, despairing of bringing about change in the world, they are no longer able to imagine alternative possibilities. They do not experience social lacks and deficiencies as intrusions or obstacles. Having withdrawn "into themselves," they no longer inhabit a resisting world.

There is a difference between those who unquestioningly accede to the given and those who find refuge in that way. In both cases, however, there is an incapacity to look at actualities as if they could be otherwise, as there is an unwillingness to try to transcend determinacy or surpass facticity. Consciousness, it so happens, involves the capacity to pose questions to the world, to reflect on what is presented in experience. It is not to be understood as an interiority. Embodied, thrusting into the lived and perceived, it opens out to the common. Human consciousness, moreover, is always situated; and the situated person, inevitably engaged with others, reaches out and grasps the phenomena surrounding him/her from a particular vantage point and against a particular background consciousness. For Merleau-Ponty, the background is to be found in a "primordial landscape" laid down and patterned by perception in the early days of life. For him, that lived, pre-reflective landscape is the foundation for the meanings that are layered or sedimented once human beings move into the life of language and begin thematizing or symbolizing their worlds (1964, pp. 13–27). There are connections between what underlies rationality for Merleau-Ponty and what Michael Polanyi called "tacit awareness" (1964, pp. 95–100). There are connections, too, with what Hans-Georg Gadamer calls "understanding," also a primordial way of being in the world (1977, pp. 18–58).

On the ground of the pre-reflective landscape or understanding, the individual develops or learns to take a variety of perspectives on the world. The perspectives available are always partial. The individual sees profiles, aspects of the building entered in the morning, the school or the agency. He/she, similarly, grasps aspects of the novel being read, the painting being looked at; there is always more to be discovered, each time he/she focuses attention. As important, each time he/she is with others—in dialogue, in teaching–learning situations, in mutual pursuit of a project—additional new perspectives open; language opens possibilities of seeing, hearing, understanding. Multiple interpretations constitute multiple realities; the "common" itself becomes multiplex and endlessly challenging, as each person reaches out from his/her own ground toward what might be, should be, is not yet.

It is with a vision of this sort that I choose to explore the problem of freedom and the diverse experiences of freedom to be found in our history, in our literature, in our collective memory. Doing so, I hope to develop a view of education for freedom that will take into account our political and social realities as well as the human condition itself. I hope to communicate a sense of things that is neither contemplative or self-regarding, a mood in which new initiatives can be imagined and dimensions of experience transformed. It is, actually, in the process of effecting transformations that the human self is created and re-created. Dewey, like the existentialist thinkers, did not believe that the self was ready-made or pre-existent; it was, he said, "something in continuous formation through choice of action" (1916, p. 408). The richness, the complexity of the selves people create are functions of their commitments to projects of action they recognize as their own. As Sartre saw it, human beings create themselves by going beyond what exists, by trying to bring something into being. There is, however, no orientation to bringing something into being if there is no awareness of something lacking in a situation. The lacks, as we have seen, may be due to what has happened in the past, to injustices in the present, to the deficits and discomforts associated with being alive at a particular time and place. They may be due to unreflectiveness, to the incapacity to interpret lived situations. It seems evident that all this holds relevance for a conception of education—if education is conceived as a process of futuring, of releasing persons to become different, of provoking persons to repair lacks and to take action to create themselves. Action signifies beginnings or the taking of initiatives; and, in education, beginnings must be thought possible if authentic learning is expected to occur.

In moving through this introduction, I have sketched a social reality in which the existence and the uses of freedom in its negative sense are continually affirmed, while at the same time Americans seem to be absorbed into a passive, consuming audience. Certain people live out this negative freedom in a persistent "lightness of being"; others seek shelter in private enclaves or what they think of as their interior lives; still others, assured of their endowment, accede or strive, on their own, for "success." All of these tendencies, as I view them, are antithetical to what I have called education for freedom. They are antithetical because they alienate persons from their own landscapes, because they impose a fallacious completeness on what is perceived. Instead of reaching out, along with others, toward open possibilities in experience, individuals in all groups accept existing structures as given. They may try to make use of them or escape them or move around them or make a mockery of them; but they feel themselves in some way doomed to see them as objective "realities," impervious to transformation, hopelessly *there*. To objectify in this fashion, to separate oneself as "subject" from an independently existent "object," is to sacrifice the possibility of becoming the "author" of one's world; and the consciousness of authorship has much to do with the consciousness of freedom.

Authorship does not imply invention *ex nihilo*. Nor does it imply the composition of texts or scripts in some space apart from the common world. The term carries with it the feeling of temporality, the sense of being in communication, the awareness of perspective in a constructed world. Human beings, of course, devise their life projects in time—against their own life histories and the wider human history into which those histories feed. They do so by means of language or a series of symbol systems that provide a mode of articulation, of ordering and expressing what is lived. To be aware of authorship is to be aware of situationality and of the relation between the ways in which one interprets one's situation and the possibilities of action and of choice. This means that one's "reality," rather than being fixed and predefined, is a perpetual emergent, becoming increasingly multiplex, as more perspectives are taken, more texts are opened, more friendships are made.

We shall explore in the pages to come ways in which freedom has been understood and acted on in our history. We will see the Enlightenment vision, with which our country began, lose its grounding in a cosmic order. We will find inherited beliefs challenged in the shadows of new factories, in bank vaults, in railroad terminals, in lonely villages, as well as in classrooms. We will watch strangers arriving, generation after generation, as boundaries of old communities are breached. And we will feel the fears of disorder, pay heed to the defenses raised, attend to those who struggle for fresh air.

This book is in no sense the first to try to reawaken the consciousness of possibility. It will not be the first to seek a vision of education that brings together the need for wide-awakeness with the hunger for community, the desire to know with the wish to understand, the desire to feel with the passion to see. I am aware of the pluralism in this country, the problem of special interests, the dissonances and enmities. I am aware of the ambivalences with respect to equality and with respect to justice as well. Fundamentally, perhaps, I am conscious of the tragic dimension in every human life. Tragedy, however, discloses and challenges; often, it provides images of men and women on the verge. We may have reached a moment in our history when teaching and learning, if they are to happen meaningfully, must happen on the verge. Confronting a void, confronting nothingness, we may be able to empower the young to create and re-create a common world—and, in cherishing it, in renewing it, discover what it signifies to be free.

CHAPTER 2

American Paradox, American Quest

Uncertain though people may be about the meanings of freedom, inattentive though they may be to what it entails, no one can deny that a concern for freedom is a leitmotiv of our time. The causes are various: dictatorship, foreign occupation, religious persecution, racial discrimination, interference with freedom of speech, apartheid. The modes of seeking liberation differ, along with the means of resistance. What is common to all is a determination to act (sometimes at any cost) against what is experienced as oppression, coercion, injustice, exclusion, neglect. The watchword for most is indeed freedom; but the meanings vary almost infinitely. There are religious definitions, nationalist ones, economic and political ones. On occasion, moral criteria are sought. A dissident somewhere will engage in a hunger strike to win the freedom to speak or to move, or to change a policy, or to witness for the sake of others. Nameless people somewhere else will govern themselves according to a theology of liberation and make sacrifices for the subjugated and the poor. Resistants will come together and sign a charter asking for free speech in a state that threatens them with imprisonment for doing so. Urban guerillas, challenging what they view as total repression, will engage in violent acts in the name of freedom. Impassioned youth, acting for a faith or for a sect, will undertake terrorist acts for the same cause. It has become nearly impossible to associate freedom as goal and *desideratum* with any transcultural or universal concept of what is right or good.

At once, it becomes increasingly difficult to make universal claims about the human desire for freedom. Innumerable cultures of "silence" (Freire, 1970, p. 80) still exist; there are numbed, hungry, and compliant populations everywhere. We can think back to the Grand Inquisitor's claim that it is cruel to offer human beings the gift of freedom; since they prefer "peace, and even death, to freedom of choice in the knowledge of good and evil" (Dostoevsky, 1879–80/ 1945, p. 302). They would sacrifice freedom for bread and happiness at any time; they know the value of submission; they know the happiness it brings. There have been numerous examples since Dostoevsky's day of what the Inquisitor had in mind. We need only think back to Erich Fromm's *Escape from Freedom* (1941), that account of the wish to dominate and enslave, of the acquiescence of others to domination and slavery. The Fascists and the Nazis were successful for years in promising security and glory to their people; and masses readily gave up their democratic liberties to gain what appeared to be higher, more sustaining goods.

Another instance of compliance (albeit of a different kind) can be found in Paul Nizan's novel, *Antoine Bloyé* (1973). Antoine is a railroad worker's son who, by playing the "wide monkey," wins a prize at a regional contest for secondary schools in France at the start of this century. After graduation, he attempts to read a book he received as a prize for scholarship.

> It is *Le Devoir* by M. Jules Simon, of the Académie Française; he opens it at random.
> "Man is free," he reads, "he is ever aware of his power not to do what he does do and to do what he does not do."
> Antoine reflects on these words and on some others besides. He ill understands them. Is his father free not to be poor, not to work nights, not to go where he does go? Is his mother free not to have her back ache from work, not to be tired out and old before her time? He himself—in what way is he free? To be free means simply not to be poor and not always ordered about. The rich enjoy a kind of freedom. People with an income. . . . He shuts M. Jules Simon's gilt-edged book never to open it again. (p. 54)

There are many such instances in history and literature, instances of people who feel themselves to be determined by outside forces or by some nameless fatality, and who feel hopelessly isolated from a world where people coming together might bring change.

This can and does occur in American society, as more and more people are absorbed in commodification, regulated by bureaucracies, deprived of participation in a public space. The great difference is that freedom is still taken to be a given in this country: to be an American is to be endowed with freedom, whether or not one acts on it or fights for it or does anything with it. An American Antoine Bloyé today would probably feel that his parents' poverty and fatigue represented infringements on their rights, erosions of their endowment. And he might comfort himself, as many Americans still do, with an evocation of an old myth—"for example, the myth of the frontier, of the perpetual new beginning, the future as boundlessly open to self-creation" (Taylor, 1985, p. 112). It is unlikely, given present circumstances, that he would try to come together with others to transform the lives they lived in common.

This attitude is in many ways encouraged by official discourse, in part where foreign policy is concerned. The United States presents itself as the apostle of freedom. It resides in our tradition, the world is told; it lies at the core of the American dream. In schools, in textbooks, in the Pledge of Allegiance, freedom (or liberty) is a taken-for-granted possession. Born into it, the young are expected to defend it, whether or not it means anything in their personal lives. Their government, in the meantime, making its own selective determinations, describes itself as the guarantor of freedom everywhere. Any movement is to be thought of as a movement of "freedom fighters" just so long as it defines itself as non-Communist or anti-Communist; since Communism, in its Soviet embodiment, is officially viewed as the chief obstacle to human freedom everywhere. Communism—meaning un-freedom—is used to summon up images of prison camps, drab populations, menacing figures in overcoats, a threatening red star. "Anti-Christ," "evil," or simply "enemy," it is associated with faceless repression and with mysterious tentacles reaching toward our boundaries. Whether or not the metaphors connect in any signal way with the social realities of the Soviet Union (which are, at the very least, more differentiated than the official rhetoric makes them seem), the view reinforces the idea of negative freedom. Not for the first time, the conservative attachment to such a notion meshes with the libertarian enthusiasm for freedom as the absence of all state interventions and controls. This, in turn, feeds a general taken-for-grantedness with respect to personal and civic liberties. It makes it possible to replace social compassion with an insistence on each person's capacity and responsibility (and freedom) to "make it" on his or her own.

Self-reliance, independence: These are part of our legacy, many believe, if they think about it at all. It is sometimes forgotten that the American Revolution and the so-called war for independence it involved were carried out, not so much in the name of freedom, but to make freedom possible on these shores. Granting the fact that the merchants and artisans saw the colonial mercantile policies and taxation practices as unwarranted infringements on their God-given rights to own (and control) their own property and to pursue wealth, they did not necessarily experience them as attacks on their personal self-determination or autonomy, except for those few who were (as Jefferson wrote in the Declaration of Independence) "taken captive on the high seas to bear arms against their country."

But how *was* freedom understood at the origin of our nation-hood? "We hold these truths to be self-evident," said the Declaration of Independence, "that all men are created equal, that they are endowed by their Creator with certain inalienable Rights, that among these are Life, Liberty and the pursuit of Happiness. That to secure these rights, Governments are instituted among Men, deriving their just powers from the consent of the governed" (Jefferson, 1776/1972, pp. 28–29). The point, of course, was that the colonial government was not securing those rights and did not any longer derive its power "from the consent of the governed." The political language of John Locke and Jean-Jacques Rousseau, along with other eighteenth-century thinkers, shaped Jefferson's discourse from the beginning, as did his classical erudition. The Greek *polis* was in many ways his paradigm: Freedom would be achieved and maintained to the extent that rational and autonomous men would come together in speech and action. John Dewey made the point that "Jefferson was not an 'individualist' in the sense of the British laissez faire liberal school" and quoted Jefferson to the effect that "man was created for social intercourse" (1940, p. 24). For Jefferson, the New World (*his* world) was one populated by independent freeholders, supported by the fruits of their own labor. Each one, he said, could be conceived as a "rational animal," attuned to the ordered universe that surrounded humankind, to Nature and to Nature's God. Possibilities existed in this country, Jefferson believed, that were unthinkable in Europe, where he had seen surging and ignorant masses, hopelessly exploited and oppressed. Independent craftsmen and property-owners, unlikely to be submerged into a collective, could come together in village squares and meeting halls and articulate their concerns in such a way as to constitute a live, consequential public sphere. It should be clear that, as Jefferson saw it, the concept of freedom was associated with a concept of action. It was neither privatist nor subjective; it could only be maintained out in the open among self-directing (and self-supporting) persons.

The great evil, for Jefferson, was "tyranny over the mind of man" (1800/1950, p. 526), the tyranny of superstition, ignorance, and external constraint or control. This conviction nurtured Jefferson's belief in education and "the general diffusion of knowledge." The means of preventing the tyrannical exercise of power, he thought, was the illumination of "the minds of the people at large" (1779/1972, p. 83 ff.). The system he proposed was a selective system, guaranteeing three years of free schooling to all children. After three years, a boy "of the best genius" would be chosen from each primary school to go to grammar school; later, "the best genius of the whole" would be kept on for six years "and the residue dismissed. By this means twenty of the best geniuses will be raked from the rubbish annually, and be instructed at public expense, so far as grammar schools go" (p. 94). After that, half of those chosen for their superiority of "parts and disposition" would go to university for three years, leaving the grammar school graduates to act as teachers in the lower schools and the graduates of the lower schools at least literate enough to vote for those who would represent them properly. "By that part of our plan which prescribes the selection of the youths of genius from among the classes of the poor," Jefferson went on, "we hope to avail the state of those talents which nature has sown as liberally among the poor as the rich, but which perish without use, if not sought for and cultivated.—But of all the views of this law none is more important, none more legitimate than that of rendering the people the safe, as they are the ultimate, guardians of their own liberty" (p. 96). Jefferson meant that without instruction, potentialities are not realized; without the opportunity to realize themselves as thinking beings, "the classes of the poor" would never be able to select the enlightened leadership needed by the republic nor to recognize corruption or the excesses of power. The argument for education, like the argument for freedom, did not touch on the satisfaction of personal desire or need. Rather, it had to do with the survival of the republic, which presumably offered all its citizens the chance to play a part, to be autonomous, to speak for themselves.

Although his approach to education was selective and hierarchical, and although he planted the seeds of what we have come to know as a meritocratic system, it must be stressed that Jefferson found in the "diffusion of knowledge" the best guarantee of the public liberties essential for the republican way of life. This was because education could prevent "tyranny over the mind of man" by reducing ignorance, allaying superstition, and loosening the bonds of external controls. He did not take into account the structural forces inherent in an increasingly complex socio-economic system or the determinants in the human psyche itself. He did not pay heed to the crippling effects of poverty and exclusion. He did not even come to terms with the impacts of industrialization and urbanization on the public space where freedom, in his view, was to be achieved. Eventually recognizing the fact that he could not prevent the coming of manufacturing to these shores, he admitted that he could not anticipate the consequences.

Nevertheless, for all the dissonance between his view of a state small enough to become a *polis* and the vast, centralized order soon to emerge, for all his agrarianism and his use of the freeholder as paradigm, he bequeathed to us a remarkable conception of the relation between freedom and the public happiness. Also, he left a notion of the connection between freedom and action too frequently ignored when people turn to him for validation of a self-regarding individualism. It is interesting to note that Alexis de Tocqueville, writing in 1840 about his visit to America several years before, said that the effects of individualism are best combatted by free institutions. Despotism, he said, relied on keeping men apart and suspicious of one another. "When the members of a community are forced to attend to public affairs, they are necessarily drawn from the circle of their own interests and snatched at times from self-observation. As soon as a man begins to treat of public affairs in public, he begins to perceive that he is not so independent of his fellow men as he had at first imagined, and that in order to obtain their support he must often lend them his cooperation" (1840/1954, II, p. 109).

De Tocqueville, however, was also deeply concerned about the effect of "manufactures" on American democracy, because of the division of labor associated with factory production, the growing dependence of factory workers, the increasing distance between those workers and their wealthy, energetic "masters." A harsh kind of aristocracy would develop, he believed, one that would enervate, stifle, and stultify the common man (1840/1954, II, p. 171). Eroding autonomy and independence as well as ordinary human relationships, it could not but eat away at the roots of freedom. By the time de Tocqueville wrote those words, the industrial revolution was clanging on its way in the United States. Its arrival and its impact may have been most dramatically communicated by Mark Twain,

writing half a century later, when he described the steamboat chug-
ging up the river in *The Adventures of Huckleberry Finn*. Huck and Jim,
having found themselves drifting south again, are on the raft at
night in a gray mist. They hear the steamboat and they light a
lantern, judging "she would see it."

> We could hear her pounding along, but we didn't see her good till she
> was close. She aimed right for us. Often they do that and try to see how
> close they can come without touching; sometimes the wheel bites off a
> sweep, and then the pilot sticks his head out and laughs, and thinks he's
> mighty smart. Well, here she comes, and we said she was going to try
> and shave us; but she didn't seem to be sheering off a bit. She was a big
> one, and she was coming in a hurry, too, looking like a black cloud with
> rows of glowworms around it; but all of a sudden she bulged out, big
> and scary, with a long row of wide-open furnace doors shining like red-
> hot teeth, and her monstrous bows and guards hanging right over us.
> There was a yell at us, and a jingling of bells to stop the engines, a pow-
> wow of cussing, and whistling of steam—and as Jim went overboard on
> one side and I on the other, she come smashing straight through the
> raft. (1885/1959, p. 98)

Huck describes his stay underwater for a minute-and-a-half and how
he bounced up for air. And then he says, "Of course that boat started
her engines again ten seconds after she stopped them, for they never
cared much for raftsmen; so now she was churning along up the
river, out of sight in the thick weather, though I could hear her."

It is not only that Huck and Jim, in the oldest American tradition, were taking action to escape from oppression—being "all
cramped up" by village pieties and hypocrisy, being enslaved by
Christians always willing to profit from a sale. They had created a
small semblance of the traditional American community: They had
come to know each other and have regard for each other as human
beings in the course of their journey. For all the insidiousness of the
slaveholding mentality and the "cash nexus" linked to it, they were
in the process of overcoming separation when the steamboat
("smashing through the raft") split them apart. The steamboat itself
is not merely a terrible image of the new technology, not merely a
metaphor for the cruel indifference of mechanical advance. It represents a force that is in many ways unknowable and irresistable; and
the experience of it could not but put the problem of freedom in a
new light.

It was, after all, one thing to feel oneself to be an independent
agent sustained by Nature and natural laws. It was quite another to

feel oneself buffeted and battered by forces one could scarcely see or understand, much less control. Granted, the election of Andrew Jackson in 1828 had opened the suffrage to great masses of white men; granted, the so-called "common man" was establishing his place on the political stage. This meant, of course, a gradual replacement of whatever *polis* survived by what we now think of as "politics"; a patronage system; backroom caucuses; struggles among special interests; a rhetoric of incitement and persuasion very different from the discourse of norm-governed debate. Popular liberties were expressed by a movement through all sorts of once-closed doors: into the White House (with muddy feet) when Jackson was inaugurated; into theatre galleries (smelling of whiskey and garlic); into neighborhoods and gardens ordinary men and women had scarcely seen before. More significantly, ordinary people had opportunities to stand for office, to seek appointment to political posts. Many acted on what they felt to be a novel freedom by moving from the stability of farm life to the cities, "before the mast," out west. Some became peddlers on the city streets, clerks, apprentices. Many, moving into the tenements now clustering around the factories, went to work side by side with immigrants as operatives in the dark, oppressive shops; some kept moving on to other places, other jobs; a few rose slowly through the system. Not atypical was the story of Lucy Larcom, who went to work in the Lowell cotton mills at the age of eleven. She became one of the Lowell "mill girls," soon widely heralded as exemplars of healthy, virtuous, benevolently ruled factory workers. "One great advantage," Lucy Larcom wrote, "which came to these many stranger girls through being brought together away from their homes, was that it taught them to go out of themselves and enter into the lives of others" (Cott, 1972, p. 128). Home life, she thought, was narrowing in contrast; women were petty "and unthoughtful of any except their own family's interests." It soon turned out that life at Lowell was not so idyllic as was claimed. The women there undertook a futile effort to petition for a ten-hour workday—and an equally futile effort to enlist their male co-workers' cooperation in an effort to improve conditions. The restlessness, even the adventurousness that had led so many young women to abandon domesticity for a more liberated existence, was abruptly tamped down; and it was not long before black wagons had to venture into the countryside to gather up mill girls, each "with a commander who is paid one dollar a head for all the girls he brings to market and more in proportion to the distance—if they bring them from a distance they cannot easily get back" (Tyler, 1944/1962, p. 213).

In many respects, this is the underside of American freedom in the nineteenth century, the consequence of a *laissez-faire* system that gave free rein to steamboat captains who "never cared much for raftsmen" and to mill owners who never cared much for "girls." Herman Melville, in a story called "The Tartarus of Maids," described a paper mill that may have been suggested by a Lowell cotton mill or some other mill dominated by machinery of a "ponderous, elaborate sort." There are blank-faced "girls" in that paper mill, "sheet-white girls"; and the narrator speaks of his horror at the sight of them and his dread before the intricate machinery, which frightens him "as some living, panting Behemoth might." He goes on: "But what made the thing I saw so specially terrible to me was the metallic necessity, the unbudging fatality which governed it" (1949, p. 209). Children also worked in such places; men, especially in the northeast, accommodated themselves to brutal conditions and to similar machines. For many, coming from squalid farms or famine-haunted Irish villages, the situation could somehow be endured. For many, wrongly or rightly, there was hope for moving up, for moving on. At once, perhaps ironically, the very expansion of such manufacturing, the advance of the industrial revolution, multiplied options for numbers of people. Old fixities were constantly dislodged; options (at least for the well nourished and the energetic) increased.

Free enterprise, as is well known, was rampant. Frontiers were conquered daily in the markets, in the financial centers, on construction sites where railroads and canals were being built. For the powerful, for the inventive, there was an apotheosis of what was thought to be freedom. Thousands moved west: scouts, trappers, cattle-drovers, finally settlers in the "virgin land" (Smith, 1950/1959). There were descriptions, documentary and fictional, of lonely people, reckless, violent, or greedy people defiant of communal rules and bonds. The images of untrammeled freedom were threatening enough to move evangelists and missionaries to send emissaries to the border towns, young men equipped with tracts and bibles meant to tamp down asocial energies. Horace Mann, at the end of his first year as secretary of the Massachusetts Board of Education in 1837, talked about the ways in which "free institutions multiply human energies." Human faculties, he said, burst forth "with uncontrollable impetuosity" in a republic. Since its institutions give greater scope to the "lower" faculties, to the love of gain, to knavery, to fraud, to unbridled ambition, deliberate action had to be taken to ensure control of the passions by morality and intelligence.

But if this is ever done, it must be mainly done during the docile and teachable years of childhood. . . . Wretched, incorrigible, demoniac, as any human being may ever have become, there was a time when he took the first step in error and in crime; when, for the first time, he just nodded to his fall, on the brink of ruin. Then, here he was irrecoverably lost, ere he plunged into the abyss of infamy and guilt, he might have been recalled, as it were, by the waving of the hand. Fathers, mothers, patriots, Christians! it is this very hour of peril through which our children are now passing." (1838/1964, p. 150)

This response to the excesses of freedom became part of the argument for the establishment of a common school.

In his reports, it is true, Mann talked about independence and self-control, and about giving people the means to resist the selfishness of others. He wrote:

It does better than to disarm the poor of their hostility to the rich; it prevents being poor. Agrarianism is the revenge of poverty against wealth. The wanton destruction of the property of others,—the burning of hay-ricks and corn-ricks, the demolition of machinery, because it supersedes hand-labor, the sprinkling of vitriol on rich dresses—is only agrarianism run mad. Education prevents both the revenge and the madness. On the other hand, a fellow-feeling for one's class or caste is the common instinct of hearts not wholly sunk in selfish regards for person or for family. The spread of education, by enlarging the cultivated class or caste, will open a wider area over which the social feelings will expand; and, if this education should be universal and complete, it would do more than all things to obliterate factitious distinctions in society. (1848/1979, p. 87)

Indeed, Mann believed that education could stop the tendency to "the domination of capital and the servility of labor," since no intelligent body of men could be permanently poor. Acknowledgment of the moral law, self-control, and the kind of intelligence needed for the maintenance of republican government: These would protect against bigotry, violence, and profligacy. Such evils, like the "anarchy" always threatening the sanctity of institutions, were incipient in a free society; and the young had to be deliberately (and universally) "trained" if these evils were to be contained.

On the one hand, Mann's view of excess and profusion evokes that line at the end of Scott Fitzgerald's *The Great Gatsby* about the "green breast" and the "vanished trees" of the new world—"the trees that had made way for Gatsby's house, had once pandered in whispers to the last and greatest of all human dreams" (1926/1953, p. 182). ("Pander" means to pimp for, to procure for. "Gatsby's house" in its vulgar, pink extravagance is the veritable exemplar of excess, profusion, and knavery as well.) The vast spaces in this country, the sense of endless possibility, "the service of a vast, vulgar, and meretricious beauty," which Gatsby saw to be "His Father's business" (p. 99), all could not but unleash energies seldom given expression on earth before. And, indeed, for many, this was—and is—what freedom has signified in this world. On the other hand, that view, with all its threatening and amoral overtones, has agitated the religious "right" today and in former days. Fearful of chaos and disorder, the spokespersons for such movements warn of damnation and demand censorship, severity, controls.

In the same years as Horace Mann's reports (and of reform movements of many kinds in the eastern states), Ralph Waldo Emerson was calling for self-reliance and resistance to bland conformity. He was fully aware of the effects of "Trade" and materialism and the reliance on property. "Society everywhere is in conspiracy against the manhood of every one of its members. Society is a joint-stock company, in which the members agree, for the better securing of his bread to each shareholder, to surrender the liberty and culture of the eater. The virtue in most request is conformity" (1841/1966, pp. 105–106). Treating individuals in the aggregate—as groups or classes—was, like attempts to impose controls from without, an undermining of freedom. "The spirit of the American freeman is already suspected to be timid, imitative, tame. Public and private avarice make the air we breathe thick and fat. The scholar is decent, indolent, complaisant" (1837/1966, p. 100). Personal freedom could be gained only through the use of intuition and imagination; it required the capacity to bridge between the immediacy of each moment to the Divine, the "Over-soul." Through "naming," through "seeing," through his/her own spontaneous effort, the individual could come in touch with the transcendent wholeness of the ideal. Freedom had to do, then, with a commitment to the ideal, with regeneration, with self-reliance, and with the eventual attainment of a communion with other souls. Unlike Horace Mann and other public figures, of course, Emerson was only minimally concerned with the social order or with reform or protection of whatever order existed. For him, the good society could emerge only when persons began reaching out for their own integrity, when they could say, as individuals, "We will walk on our own feet; we will work with our own hands; we will speak our own minds" (p. 100).

The question of whether freedom can be achieved apart from institutions and social arrangements will continue to preoccupy us, as it has preoccupied reformers and educators over the years. Even now we cannot but ask ourselves whether Emerson could have made himself understood by Lucy Larcom or the other mill girls at the Lowell mills. Could he have made himself heard by the "sheet-white girls," by the men on the docks, by the steamboat captains, by the Jay Goulds and the Commodore Vanderbilts and the Gatsbys of the new world? Henry David Thoreau, in his turn, saw the greed for gold and the concern for power and abstract ideals to be antithetical to freedom. "Even if we grant that the American has freed himself from a political tyrant," he wrote, "he is still the slave of an economical and moral tyrant. . . . What is it to be born free and not to live free? What is the value of any political freedom, but as a means to moral freedom? Is it a freedom to be slaves, or a freedom to be free of which we boast?" ("Life Without Principle," 1863/1957, pp. 323–324). The whole point of establishing a *res-publica*, Thoreau said, was to make sure nothing happened to the *res-privata*, the private state. He was not interested in government and legislation; he was indifferent to politics. He thought politics (comparatively "superficial and inhuman") should be performed unconsciously, like the functions of the human body.

Walden, it is true, is a potent challenge to readers to awaken, to act to achieve their own freedom, to choose the terms on which they will associate with others. Far more than Emerson, Thoreau showed concern for the poor. He knew that "the luxury of one class is counterbalanced by the indigence of another. On the one side is the palace, on the other are the almshouse and the 'silent poor'" (Thoreau, 1854/1963, pp. 24–25). He noticed the shanties along the railroads, the unlit "sties" where so many lived, the contracted bodies due to "shrinking from cold and misery." But he appeared to think that if the wealthy and the "herd" that imitated them would realize that most of their luxuries were superfluous, if everyone would decide to lead a simple, even a primitive, life, there would not exist such extremes between classes. There would be no need to exploit others if the advantaged ones would stop indulging and exploiting themselves. At the end of *Walden*, there is talk of ice melting and reawakening and rebirth. "Who knows what beautiful and winged life, whose egg has been buried for ages under many concentric layers of woodenness in the dead dry life of society . . . heard perchance gnawing out now for years by the astonished family of man, as they sat around the festive board—may unexpectedly come forth from amidst society's most trivial and handselled furniture, to enjoy its perfect summer life at last?" (p. 252). All depended on the autonomy and heightened consciousness of the individual; there was no suggestion of individuals coming together in a public space to bring freedom into existence. There was only a metaphor for a *natural* emergence among human beings refusing ant-like lives, acquiescence, and conformity.

The metaphor, the sense of possibility remain potent, if we can free them from the sedimentations of cliché. Thoreau's appeal was to the consciousness of personal agency, so often obliterated by thoughtlessness or by accommodation to a system or submergence in the crowd. Without the consciousness of agency, no human being is likely to take the initiative needed for the achievement of freedom. For Thoreau, however, his writing and his abolitionism exhausted his urge to action. Both *Walden* and *On Civil Disobedience* still function as potential pedagogies in the sense that they aim at raising the consciousness of those willing to pay heed. Perhaps we can view Thoreau in the company of utopian socialists like Robert Owen, Frances Wright, and Robert Dale Owen as harbingers of an alternative tradition in this country, for all the tension between their points of view, the fragility of their dreams.

A novelist, however, seemed at the time to be most eloquent in pointing out the relationship between human connection and the desire for freedom. We need only recall Hester Prynne in Nathaniel Hawthorne's *The Scarlet Letter*. The novel deals, of course, with Puritan times; but it was written in the mid-nineteenth century, and the reality created is in part the stuff of Hawthorne's lived experience, in part a function of a social reality shared with Emerson and Thoreau. Hester, ostracized after her imprisonment for the "sin" of adultery, goes to live in an abandoned cottage on the outskirts of town, there to bring up in solitude her little daughter Pearl. In her loneliness, Hester's life turns "from passion and feeling to thought."

> It was an age in which the human intellect, newly emancipated, had taken a more active and a wider range than for many centuries before. Men of the sword had overthrown nobles and kings. Men bolder than these had overthrown and rearranged—not actually, but within the sphere of theory, which was their most real abode—the whole system of ancient prejudice, wherewith was linked much of ancient principle. Hester Prynne imbibed this new spirit. She assumed a freedom of speculation, then common enough on the other side of the Atlantic, but which our forefathers, had they known of it, would have held to be a deadlier crime than that stigmatized by the scarlet letter. In her lone-

some cottage by the sea-shore, thoughts visited her, as dared to enter no other dwelling in New England. (1850/1969, p. 183)

Hester conforms with a cold, controlled demeanor to what society asks of her; but she does so only because she has a responsibility for her child. Otherwise, Hawthorne commented, she might have become, like Ann Hutchison, foundress of a religious sect, or been sentenced to death for trying "to undermine the foundations of the Puritan establishment." Unlike Thoreau, and for all the limits placed on her by parenthood, she appears to believe that freedom in itself is meaningless unless it brings changes about in the world. Moreover, she feels despairing and alienated in her emancipated condition; there is something disturbing about looking from an estranged point of view "at human institutions, and whatever priests or legislators had established; criticizing with hardly more reverence than the Indian would feel for the clerical band, the judicial robe, the pillory, the gallows, the fireside, or the church" (p. 217). Her separation does not fill her with "creative elan" and offer the joyous sense of personal rebirth. It chills her; it distorts her personality. Strong as she is, she experiences a kind of shame until she finds connection once again with Dimmesdale and then (as "good Samaritan") among the citizens of the town.

Hester disappears after Dimmesdale's death. There is word that she has traveled far, that Pearl has made a wealthy marriage. Suddenly, Hester reappears at her old cottage. She has no "selfish ends"; people come to her for counsel and advice, women especially. She does what she can for them and assures them that in some brighter period the relation between men and women would be established "on a surer ground for mutual happiness" (p. 275). She seems to realize that her freedom and that of others could be finally and significantly realized only in association with others as they came together in the making of a better world. She knows she will not be the one to bring it into being; but her emancipation has enabled her to link her own freedom to a kind of social commitment, to a vision rare enough in a period of great and untrammelled individualism. Yes, there were a few others in actuality: the Grimké sisters, for instance, who left their wealthy southern family to work for abolition and women's rights; former slaves like Frederick Douglass; the women who organized the Women's Rights convention at Seneca Falls. Here and there, resistance to oppression and exclusion was taking political form in the old Jeffersonian sense: Persons, presumed to be rational, were engaging in public debate in spheres they opened for themselves.

The Civil War was preceded by talk of freedom, of course, by such devices as "liberty rules" in the northern states, which were to prevent people from returning escaped slaves to the south, by fruitless efforts to persuade or coerce slaveowners to free their own slaves in the name of human rights, by varied challenges to efforts to extend slavery into the new territories of the west. As is generally known by now, the primary cause of the Civil War was not a desire to free the slaves; the tension between the industrialism of the north and the agrarianism of the south was far more significant, as was the desire to protect the Union when the slave states threatened to secede. The victory of industrialism, trade, and capitalism led not only to a "Gilded Age" of *laissez-faire* and triumphant, often exploitative, individualism. The Fourteenth Amendment to the Constitution, treating corporations as persons and holding them immune from government regulation, made a mockery of the idea of negative freedom—freedom *from* interference and control. The way was prepared for the "robber barons," those inventive enough to organize business into larger and larger units, to make fortunes for themselves, to justify by an ideology of success.

Melville's Captain Ahab in *Moby Dick* still serves as exemplar of that sort of freedom, giving license to dominate by exercise of will, no matter what the cost to those in the mines and factories, those making up the *Pequod*'s crew. "What I've dared, I've willed; and what I've willed, I'll do," says Ahab. ". . . Swerve me? ye cannot swerve me, else ye swerve yourselves! . . . The path to my fixed purpose is laid with iron rails, whereon my soul is grooved to run. Over unsounded gorges, through the rifled hearts of mountains, under torrents' beds, unerringly I rush! Naught's an obstacle, naught's an angle to the iron way !" (1851/1981, p. 172). He is addressing himself to the forces of nature, to his fellowmen, to his crew. He has to use tools to accomplish his purpose, Melville wrote, "and of all tools used in the shadow of the moon, men are most apt to set out of order." He thinks that, in order to keep them loyal on the manic journey, he must not strip them "of all hopes of cash—aye, cash. They may scorn cash now; but let some months go by, and no prospective promise of it to them, and then this same quiescent cash all at once mutinying in them, this same cash would cashier Ahab" (p. 216). Like the factory-owners and the financiers, Ahab will pay as little as possible, in accord with what is considered each man's contribution to the final product, if there were a final product and not a fated pursuit of a White Whale. This is his freedom, his total freedom from constraint and control. And it is emblematic. When the ship is finally wrecked by the giant whale, Ahab cries, "The ship! The hearse! . . . its wood could only be American" (p. 574).

Even Walt Whitman, the poet of the self, the "divine average," saw that equality and freedom had somehow to be harmonized through "loving comradeship" or "adhesiveness" (1855/1931, p. 686). But the engines of unswerving capitalism whirred on. There seemed indeed to be "iron rails" on which the souls (and heads and hands) of unconstrained businessmen were "grooved to run." It was not long before a rationale was found for this in Darwinism. The economist and sociologist William Graham Sumner, applying the doctrine of survival of the fittest to the social realm, treated *laissez-faire* as if it were as "natural" and fixed as the law of gravity. Corruption and poverty were natural processes, and nothing should be done to hinder or attenuate the survival of the fittest, who (by the very nature of capitalism) would become the builders and shapers of a society geared to production and material success (1906). It followed from this point of view that education could play no part in "improving" society, making it fairer or more humane; at best, its function was to transmit from one generation to another a proper understanding of the order of things. For the ordinary person, for the poor and submerged, any dream of freedom had to give way to adjustment to the necessary. And the necessary meant a continuation of economic development with all that it entailed in the way of invention, expansion, and the accumulation of wealth. The "opinion" of those whose labor would make this possible was of no importance. The Whitmanesque ideal of "communion" and "loving comradeship" could be realized, if at all, only in sheltered places without effect on the larger world.

On the surface, there are resemblances between the Sumnerian view and that of William Torrey Harris, philosopher, then superintendent of schools, then commissioner of education at the turn of the century. Harris, too, affirmed the values of the industrial order as an upward step in the advance of civilization; and his cognitivist, formalist approach to school curricula was grounded in the conviction that the young had to develop a rational world view in order to properly relate themselves to the world order and the institutions that gave it visible form (1900). The difference was that Harris was a Hegelian; and the Hegelian view was that "civilization" is an expression of a cosmic order founded on reason and understandable by rational minds. Only the free and autonomous person can exercise reason adequately, not the bounded or "natural" or purely "subjective" self. It follows that the recognition of a world order or a world spirit is the ultimate object of a free will; and Harris's apparently conservative conception of educating was intended as a means of releasing persons in all their diversity to become their true, rational, and autonomous selves. What remains crucial here is the connection between the attainment of freedom and the consciousness of some larger, encompassing whole; and we shall see this variously expressed in the work of other Hegelians or post-Hegelians, most particularly in the work of Marxists (or those influenced by Marx) and of John Dewey, who found his philosophical maturity in Hegelian philosophy.

For all this, we must pause to ask ourselves how the ordinary individual, experiencing the constraining pressures of factory life or of class prejudices or even the conceived determinism of what was thought of as "scientific law" or a universe modelled on a machine, thought of himself/herself in this "free country." We must assume that those in the laboring masses, for all their acquiescence to what was presented to them as "natural," experienced restive moments, rebellions against the deliberate deprivation of the power to make choices for themselves. Thinking about the thousands who worked in the steel companies and the cotton factories and on the early assembly lines at the beginning of the century, I find it hard not to summon up a searing contrast between Melville's description of the seamen on the whaling ship touched with "abounding dignity"—a dignity "shining in the arm that wields a pick or drives a spoke; that democratic dignity which, on all sides, radiates without end from God Himself" (p. 119)—and Mark Twain's rendering (in *A Connecticut Yankee*) of the technician Hank Morgan's contempt for the "human muck" he once thought he could redeem by reason and technology. It is not only the brutality and violence used in putting down the Homestead and Pullman strikes at the close of the nineteenth century; it is what that brutality and violence signified when it came to regard for the "common man," for his dignity, even for his common sense. As is generally known, the breaking of those strikes caused a long hiatus in labor organization; and this had to mean a reduced capacity to look at things as if they could be otherwise. Surely, the remedy could not have been an education in the Harris tradition, an education geared to enabling the individual to understand and accept his place in the institutional order of things. Once we include the worker in our consideration of freedom (as so few educational thinkers have done), we cannot but find the problematic intensifying.

Yes, as we shall recall in a moment, there were the progressives and the rebels against "formalism" (White, 1957), who were still affirming "that democratic dignity" and developing a conception of intelligence and social action that was to empower persons to achieve their freedom in spite of everything. But we cannot avoid the cautionary instances in the imaginative literature of the time: Clyde Griffiths in Theodore Dreiser's *An American Tragedy*, enslaved by a dream of wealth and upward mobility, by (perhaps) what had become *the* American dream; Henry Fleming in Stephen Crane's *The Red Badge of Courage*, blown back and forth, battered, and finally rewarded by giant forces he cannot name or understand. It may be Crane's *Maggie: A Girl of the Streets* that renders most fearfully the perceived impersonality of things, the exteriority of causation, the determinism in others' attitudes. Maggie, now called "the girl," is walking through the city, indifferent, closed in on herself, rejected by every man she passes. She goes into gloomy places "where the tall black factories shut in the street and only occasional broad beams of light fell across the sidewalks from saloons." And then:

> She went into the blackness of the final block. The shutters of the tall buildings were closed like grim lips. The structures seemed to have eyes that looked over them, beyond them, at other things. Afar off the lights of the avenues glittered as if from an impossible distance. Street-car bells jingled with a sound of merriment. At the feet of the tall buildings appeared the deathly black hue of the river. Some hidden factory sent up a yellow glare, that lit for a moment the waters lapping oilily against timbers. The varied sounds of life, made joyous by distance and seeming unapproachableness, came faintly and died away to a silence. (1892/1960, p. 81)

Without envisaging any alternative, Maggie drowns herself, and so it is. She is poverty-stricken, a whore, a victim, and responsible. But in no significant way is she free.

It was the 1890s, and already the reformers were beginning to stir in many fields: the courts, the writing of history; the exposure of political scandals and industrial exploitation; economics; education; psychology; and philosophy. Among the things that united such diverse individuals as Oliver Wendell Holmes, Thorstein Veblen, Vernon Louis Parrington, William James, John Dewey, Lincoln Steffens, Charles Beard, and Jane Addams was a concern for experience in the changing contexts of the country and a belief in the uses of experimental intelligence in effecting reforms. Many, as well, believed that an address to what they thought of as a democratic conscience in America would move people to take the action required to repair inequities and moral failures, to widen the space where freedom could be achieved. Not all may have gone as far as Charles Beard in pointing to the economic determinates behind the making of the Constitution and other watershed events in our history. Not all may have challenged the philosophical warranties of systems and "hard" determinisms with the pragmatic passion of a William James. Not all may have lashed out at the plutocracy and the dominance of the "pecuniary" with the acerbity of a Thorstein Veblen. But they shared a rejection of archaic abstractions and precedents; they shared a profound faith in hypothetical and empirical inquiries; and they shared an understanding of the transactional relationships between living human beings and their environments.

Where the problem, indeed the "dialectic," of freedom, was concerned, there was a dramatic shift from both the Jeffersonian and the Emersonian definitions, despite the survival of the spirit of Jeffersonian republicanism and Emersonian idealism. For one thing, there was a recognition of the insufficiency of negative freedom and of the view that freedom was an endowment. For another thing, there was a turning away from visions of the divine and the spiritual in both Emersonian and Hegelian senses. Dewey, as has been said, grew up in the Hegelian stream; and the Hegelian view of dialectical change and development remained alive in his thinking. What he rejected in time, however, was the idea of the World Spirit, the Absolute, the cosmic order. Finding different meanings in Darwinian theory than had Sumner and the so-called Social Darwinians, he found in the very notion of natural evolution suggestions for a view of open-ended development enhanced by a conception of dialectical interchange that would overcome old dualisms and discontinuities. Like the sociologist Lester Ward, he saw the human mind as a distinctive mode of adaptation to the environment in a world that was always challenging and always new. The invention of cultures was seen as a break with natural selection. Capable of thinking and choosing, capable of communicating and transmitting valued ways of life, men and women could direct the course of future evolution. No longer subject to the repetitive patterns laid down by instinct, they could be educated to pose questions, to pursue meanings, to effect changes, to extend control. Making more and more connections in their own experience, reflecting on their shared lives, taking heed of the consequences of the actions they performed, they would become aware of more and more alternatives, more and more experiential possibilities; and this meant an increased likelihood of achieving freedom. The capacity for achieving it, however, had to be continually nurtured, informed, and communally sustained. This recognition could not but feed into Dewey's articulations of a theory of experiential education and also into his descriptions of the social involvements and supports that eventually might lead to a "great society" (Dewey, 1927/1954).

The Hegelian view that autonomy and freedom are attained when human beings grasp, through the exercise of reason, the overarching order of things was revised. For Dewey, there was no cosmic purpose fulfilling itself in history. Nonetheless, there was a clear connection between identity and what he called the "freed intelligence" necessary for direction of freedom of action. Dewey wrote:

> The democratic idea of freedom is not the right of each individual to *do* as he pleases, even if it be qualified by adding "provided he does not interfere with the same freedom on the part of others." While the idea is not always, not often enough, expressed in words, the basic freedom is that of freedom of *mind* and of whatever degree of freedom of action and experience is necessary to produce freedom of intelligence. (1937/1940, p. 341)

The freedoms guaranteed in the Bill of Rights, Dewey said, were of this nature. Without them, individuals were not free to develop, "and society is deprived of what they might contribute." He knew, as did those around him in the Progressive Era, that freedom of mind and freedom of action were functions of membership and participation in some valued community. It is important to hold in mind the idea (as important for Charles Taylor, Hannah Arendt, and Jurgen Habermas as for Dewey) that the *person*—that center of choice— develops in his/her fullness to the degree he/she is a member of a live community. The distinctive optimism of the reformers in their various fields in the Progressive Era was linked to their faith that embodied "social intelligence" could, even in the midst of momentous economic changes, bring into existence such a community.

They believed they could devise a mode of social inquiry inextricably linked to their commitment to democratic norms and values. Indeed, they could not conceive of democratic freedom apart from critical thinking, hypothetical inquiry, the open exchange of ideas. Scientific planning, even types of social engineering, could be undertaken in the light of traditional American notions of freedom and dignity, which would always stand in the way of manipulation of human beings or insults to their integrity. In those days, before the vast developments in technology that made Hiroshima possible and the "scientific" extermination in the German concentration camps, it was difficult to conceive of scientific exploration and invention as harmful or hostile to humanity. They represented, as Dewey often said, intelligence working at the height of its effectiveness. They opened the way to improvements in public health, human interchange, and industrial production, even as they expanded possibilities of beneficent control. As a number of observers have remarked, it was reasonable to think this way and hope this way before science lost its "innocence" through its alliance to technologies. The crucial point was to keep as many people as possible informed about the meanings of science and the anticipated consequences of what it achieved. Again, the pivotal issue was the nurture of intelligence. Given adequate nurture, it would inform experience, stimulate the ongoing quest for meaning and purpose; it would inevitably keep democratic freedom alive.

Yes, there were numerous commentators and scholars who saw the dehumanizing forces at work in American society—the philistinism, the materialism, the power of corporate entities, what Henry James called the "money grope." Thorstein Veblen, Lincoln Steffens, Ida Tarbell, Frank Norris, and others exposed and dramatized the "pecuniary" domination of the culture, the corruption and "shame" of local governments, the imperial greed of the Sinclair Oil Company, the exploitation in the slaughterhouses and factories. They were the "muckrakers," convinced that their reports would arouse what they thought of as the "democratic conscience" and move people to take action to reform. Schools transformed (as Dewey wanted them to be) into "miniature communities"; settlement houses opened to union members as well as the immigrant poor; civic groups; neighborhood associations: Together they would (even in the face of rampant *laissez-faire*) gradually bring into being the kind of social order that might nourish identity, release human preferences, lay the ground for the full achievement of freedom by all the members of an expanding community. It must be granted that, even in a day when men like W. E. B. DuBois, Booker T. Washington, and numerous other great black leaders were making their voices audible, the reformers paid little attention to the poisons of racism, to the problem of minorities in general. This, in itself, may testify to their view that freedom ought to be thought of (at least in some cases) as an endowment or a gift. The slaves, after all, were free, Jim Crow and the Ku Klux Klan notwithstanding. What happened in the retrograde south was not one of the "shames" with which reformers need be concerned.

To write this is to recall another Melville short story, one that not only holds intimations of such well-meaning shortsightedness, but implicitly warns of the integral relation of racism to America's hopes for itself. The story is called "Benito Cereno" (1856/1952, pp. 255–353) and deals with a slave revolt on a Spanish ship in 1799. More significantly, however, it deals with the limited perceptions and prejudices of the righteous Captain Amasa Delano of Duxbury, Massachusetts, who attempts to help the ship's captain and is totally unable to see what has occurred aboard the *San Dominick*, by now totally derelict and in distress. Delano is totally convinced of his own fairness and competence. Unable to question any of his own assumptions, he takes it for granted that whites are "naturally" the masters of the dark people of the world. He looks at Babo, who turns out to have been the leader of the uprising, and sees "the most pleasing body-servant . . . one, too, whom a master need be on no silly superior terms with, but may treat with familiar trust; less a servant than a devoted companion" (p. 263). Indeed, Delano is so contemptuous of the blacks as to be unable to believe that they can act for themselves at all, much less take over a ship and disguise what they have done. He cannot acknowledge even for a moment his own nation's, his own state's complicity in the violence against black people; he cannot acknowledge the place of domination of others in the search for freedom associated with the opening of the New World. "Benito Cereno" begins with an account of a gray morning, with the sea seeming "sleeked at the surface like gray lead. . . . Flights of troubled gray fowl, kith and kin with flights of troubled gray vapors among which they were mixed, skimmed low and fitfully over the waters, as swallows over meadows before storms. Shadows present, foreshadowing deeper shadows to come" (p. 255). Near the end, the ship's captain is talking to Captain Delano in Lima before Cereno's death and Babo's voiceless execution. Delano tries to comfort Cereno by telling him to forget the past, to note how the sun and the blue sea have forgotten it. "'But these mild trades that now fan your cheek, do they not come with a human-like healing to you? Warm friends, steadfast friends are the trades.' 'With their steadfastness they but waft me to my tomb, señor,' was the foreboding response. 'You are saved,' cried Captain Delano, more and more astonished and pained; 'you are saved: what has cast such a shadow upon you?' 'The negro.'"

We are reminded by Melville of what was overlooked by the great reformers, including Dewey and Steffens, Jane Addams and Justice Brandeis: not only the sense in which nature abhors slavery, but the sense in which a free society (and its citizens) are morally endangered by unacknowledged mastery, by domination of every kind. John Schaar, writing about the story, said that disharmony (or what was once called "sin") "is the pervasive and palpable reality of everyday life." We feel it in ourselves, see it in the world, if we are at all willing to confront that world and its often nightmarish history. "Nor can we refuse to play the game. Human beings, unlike the cattle, must choose what they will do and be. We are not governed by our instincts or totally dominated by our keepers. Rather, we are free; and our freedom puts us under an imperative of decision and action. And each action is in time. It is taken on the knife-edge of the present, and thus both completes a life to that point and projects it into the future. Stories such as 'Benito Cereno' only dramatize and sharpen this quality of the human condition" (1979, p. 443).

Our knowledge is, it must be admitted, always insufficient; and that is partly why there is so much "anguish" associated with our choices, our responses to what Schaar called an "imperative." Moreover, the moral complexities of what is done are often impenetrable, particularly since we only partially understand our own motives and intentions, no matter how critically self-reflective we try to be. Also, the consequences of free action, which cannot but change our situations, are to a large degree unpredictable. Hannah Arendt has written that that unpredictability arises partly from the unreliability of human beings who can never guarantee what will happen tomorrow and from the impossibility "of foretelling the consequences of an act within a community of equals where everybody has the same capacity to act" (Arendt, 1958, p. 244). In some respect, this is the price we pay for freedom and "for plurality and reality, for the joy of inhabiting together with others a world whose reality is guaranteed for each by the presence of all."

When we think of the hopes as well as the blindness of the Progressive Era, of the fundamental unpredictability of a society or a world over which so many thought they had gained control, we cannot be surprised to recall the withering of the utopian vision during and after the First World War. The United States did not suffer as the European countries suffered in the course of the war. We did not lose so many young men; our territories were not violated; we did not have to face the terrors and repressions that followed in the wake of (or in the face of) revolutions that swept so much of the world. We did not, after a few years, have to face the ways in which rational and presumably free minds accepted and carried out the Draconian and genocidal plans made by European ideologues, dictators, chancellors, generals, leaders of all kinds. But Americans did have to confront the irrelevance of their traditional hopes and pieties. They had, some of them, to look at the blind rectitude, akin to that of which Captain Delano was so proud. Most significantly, they had to suffer the rapid decline of their Enlightenment faith in intelligence and benign control. Market forces, military forces of incalculable scale, mysterious political forces—all seemed to overwhelm the confidence in cool, intelligent planning associated with the reform ideal. We might but look again at the reforms associated with Woodrow Wilson's "New Freedom," at the Congress's rejection of membership in the League of Nations, at the overcoming of vision by the "normalcy" of the post-war presidencies.

Voices, images spring again to mind, most particularly when the fall of the utopian dreams becomes so visible. I think of Ernest Hemingway's Nick Henry—seeking a justification for a "separate peace" in *A Farewell to Arms*:

> I was always embarrassed by the words sacred, glorious, and sacrifice and the expression in vain. We had heard them, sometimes standing in the rain almost out of earshot, so that only the shouted words came through, and had read them on proclamations . . . and I had seen nothing sacred, and the things that were glorious had no glory and the sacrifices were like the stockyards at Chicago if nothing was done with the meat except to bury it. (1929/1952, p. 186)

Facing certain death, he deserts from the Italian army and makes "a separate peace." There is no hope of new possibility in a world that "kills the very good and the very gentle and the very brave impartially." The narrator concludes: "If you are none of these you can be sure it will kill you too but there will be no special hurry" (p. 252). I think of John Dos Passos writing in *The 42nd Parallel*: "They went over with the A.E.F. to save the Morgan loans, to save Wilsonian Democracy, they stood at Napoleon's Tomb and dreamed empire, they had champagne cocktails at the Ritz bar and slept with Russian countesses in Montmartre and dreamed empire, all over the country at American legion posts and business men's luncheons it was worth money to make the eagle scream; they lynched the pacifists and the proGermans and the wobblies and the reds and the bolsheviks" (1930/1936, p. 351). This is fiction; and it does not matter if it is empirically true. What matters is that this was a point of view, not Dos Passos's alone, and that it made the search for freedom and the meaning of freedom more complex than they had ever been.

After the First World War, artists expatriated themselves to seek a new kind of liberation abroad. The American dream, which had now become (in Fitzgerald's words) a dream of "vast, vulgar, and meretricious beauty" (1953, p. 99), served as justification for new pursuits of wealth, new constraints on dissident thinking, new pressures on the masses to conform. It was a time of "scientific management" and "efficiency" in education (Callahan, 1962/1964) as the schools tried to come to terms with unfamiliar crowds of children, to be sorted out somehow for the work that had to be done. Here and there, in the open space of a progressive private school, freedom was linked to spontaneity and expressiveness; only gradually did other schools come to concern themselves with social issues and the need for "social inquiry." At the end of the 1930s, Dewey was explicitly concerned with schools that lacked both manners and control, where freedom was an end in itself. Still emphasizing the crucial importance of freedom of intelligence, "that is to say, freedom of observation and of judgment exercised on behalf of purposes that are intrinsically worthwhile," Dewey went on to say that negative freedom was justified only as a means to "freedom which is power: power to frame purposes, to judge wisely, to evaluate desires by the consequences which will result from acting upon them; power to select and order means to carry chosen ends into operation" (1938/1963, p. 61). But purposes, however, could grow only through the process of social intelligence.

It was difficult to declare a "separate peace" in the New Deal period, when values grounded in a sense of solidarity were affirmed in the struggle against economic crisis. There was a brief resurgence of the utopianism of the Progressive Era in the days of *The Social Frontier*, when New Deal supporters joined with Marxist scholars to challenge the domination of high finance and to explore the role of schools when it came to bringing about desirable changes in "the social order." If there was an ideal image of freedom in those difficult times, it might be found in the familiar passage in John Steinbeck's *The Grapes of Wrath*, when Tom Joad, fugitive and "outlaw," decides to enter into a larger community to escape being driven by those who are "drivin' all our people."

> Wherever they's a fight so hungry people can eat, I'll be there. Wherever there's a cop beatin' up a guy, I'll be there. . . . I'll be in the way

guys yell when they're mad an'—I'll be in the way kids laugh when they're hungry an' they know supper's ready. An' when our folks eat the stuff they raise an' live in the houses they build—why, I'll be there. (1939, p. 573)

He may be said to be pursuing his freedom by refusing "the wall," the "impossible." He may be said to be exercising his "power" for the sake of building a new community, perhaps reconstituting an old community. At the least, he is moving beyond the limits established by resignation and helplessness. The "Golden Gate," the old frontier has been closed to him and his fellow Okies, the migrants, the excluded and persecuted ones. And so he moves out to what may be a new frontier of collective action, a people's movement that may (or may not) bring about the desperately needed change.

Tom Joad is a farmer's son and uneducated; but, in many respects, he is an exemplar of what could happen in the 1930s. Having lost hope for the traditional modes of incremental improvement, many chose to join collectivities reaching far beyond their own intimates or what was left of their own communities. For some, it meant the Socialist party; for others, the Communist movement in one or another of its phases. There is a sense in which many of the radicals of the time engaged in what Maurice Merleau-Ponty described as an existential project; they were not applying intellectual solutions to what they had defined as major social problems. As Merleau-Ponty presented it, a working man who has long taken for granted the confinements of his life may suddenly perceive that he shares a common lot with day-laborers, farm workers, and other factory workers. Doing so, he may gradually reconceive his way of co-existing with other people and begin living through an experience that might be characterized as "class-conscious." Along with others, he may find his life polarized toward a goal that can be fully "recognized only on being attained" (1962/1967, p. 446). The point has to do with freedom. A space of action seems to open before the situated person, who then makes a commitment extending toward the future. This means that he moves his own life from its ordinary spontaneous or "natural" course and, identifying himself by means of a project lived with fellow-workers, making his commitment meaningful through the actions he undertakes, then achieves what Merleau-Ponty called "conditioned freedom."

The existential projects of the 1930s, striking many people as revolutionary, were lived out in resistance to an "Americanism" that considered them threats to freedom, and in dissonance with problem-solving methodologies that led to the New Deal reforms. It will be important to recall the difference between an existential project and a program or plan deliberately carried through: an ordering of means for the accomplishment of "worthwhile" ends. Nonetheless, going back in time to the New Deal period, we find such an ordering (in, for example, the establishment of the Works Progress Administration, the arts projects, the youth employment undertakings, the Civilian Conservation Corps), creating the kinds of support systems that made freedom attainable for many who were excluded before. Perhaps one of the most potent symbolic manifestations of it can be found in the murals done in post offices with government support, in regional theatres, in health clinics. All provided spaces (through planning and the application of intelligence) in which personal freedoms could be attained in the troubled, intersubjective world. As Robert Reich now sees it, "Franklin D. Roosevelt's boldest innovation has been designating the *nation* as a community. At a time when the whole nation was stricken and only a massive common campaign could hope to prevail over depression and fascism, this designation was compelling to the American people" (1986, pp. 168–169). He also remarks that it took some 30 years before the notion of a national community became linked to the idea of welfare. We may consider, as we move on, whether an attitude of solidarity pervaded Roosevelt's national community in contrast to the altruism that prevailed in Lyndon Johnson's, and whether solidarity is more likely to feed the growth of freedom than the "benevolence" presumably characterizing the welfare state.

In any event, it seems clear enough that the very suggestion of a national community made it relatively simple to mobilize the American people for a war against fascism after the attack on Pearl Harbor. Looking back over a landscape marred by the jarring shapes of the Korean and the Vietnam wars, we believe we see a period of the most inspiring epiphanies in the Second World War. Freedom then meant everything that fascism crushed below its iron wheels: the right to speak for oneself; the right to dissent; the right to worship as one pleased; the granting of "human" rights to the "other," whoever that "other" might be. Only later, when we became aware of unpleasant, immoral, ostensibly righteous denials of holocaust in Europe, of doors closed against the stateless and the persecuted, of alliances with torturers who were "anti-Communist," did many Americans come face to face once more with the unpredictable and the morally unfathomable. And when science, now wedded to technology in the sandy flatlands of Los Alamos, presented its most sophisticated achievement to the world at Hiroshima (and when those who were responsible said, "Thank God, it worked!"), the modern problem of freedom in its association with intelligence became desperately complex. Arendt has also written about the irreversibility of the process started by free acts, as well as its unpredictability. "The possible redemption from the predicament of irreversibility—of being unable to undo what one has done though one did not, and could not, have known what he was doing—is the faculty of forgiving. The remedy for unpredictability . . . is contained in the faculty to make and keep promises" (1958, p. 237). Forgiving, she said, keeps the deeds of the past from hanging like Damocles's sword over each new generation. Being bound to the fulfillment of promises, however, enables us to keep our identities, which can be confirmed only in the presence of others—who are there to confirm the identity between the one who promises and the one who fulfills. Considering such a view, I believe it unthinkable any longer for Americans to assert themselves to be "free" because they belong to a "free" country. Not only do we need to be continually empowered to choose ourselves, to create our identities within a plurality; we need continually to make new promises and to act in our freedom to fulfill them, something we can never do meaningfully alone.

The determination to do this takes, as we have seen, diverse forms in our country. A little more than a century after the publication of Thoreau's *Walden*, the generation of the 1960s felt afflicted, diversely afflicted, by disillusionment and powerlessness. They began speaking, many of them, in tones very like Thoreau's and expressing a kindred sensibility. Most were university students, confronting bureaucracies, corporate structures, bland and usually smiling administrators. They said they felt obliterated as living persons, reduced to statistical formulations, to "IBM cards." Tom Hayden, speaking to University of Michigan students in 1962, emphasized their sense of being manipulated by unknown forces, the powerlessness they had experienced under their apparent complacency. "Do not wish to be a student," he said, "in contrast to being a man" (1967, pp. 279–80). What followed is well known, if vaguely remembered: the student unrest, the taking to the road, the mysticisms, the psychedelic experiments. We shall deal later with the civil rights movement, which sheds a different light on the problem of freedom, although it must be admitted that (especially in 1964) many who were or would be campus protesters played worthy parts in "Mississippi Summer," voter registration projects, and the rest. The clear commitments of the moment changed; but, at the time, people did come together in "speech and action." Not only did they create a fragile "in-between" among themselves; they identified a purpose, a vocation for themselves, so that freedom for them was more than an empty frame. Similar things happened here and there in the peace movement that took shape in protest against the war in Vietnam. Sometimes in small groups, sometimes in large, people made spaces for themselves, places where they could act on their indignation, places where they could identify themselves.

But the complexities and ambiguities of what turned out to be a short-lived libertarianism were manifold. Young people (ordinarily middle-class and privileged, reared to the comforts and indulgences challenged by Thoreau so many years before) sought a freedom beyond culture, or what some called a "counter-cultural" freedom. The dominant culture was seen as one (in Jules Henry's words) "against man" (1963), with a habitual insistence on using "man" as a generic term. Henry wrote: "Although it is true that the price of social acceptance is conformity and loss of freedom, that one builds a personal community by mortgaging his individuality, the tough-minded kinds who, for one reason or another, cannot fit in with the majority and are squeezed out of the conforming groups, join forces with one another, reinforcing each other's differences, gaining strength to set themselves against the majority and stimulating each other's creative elan" (p. 149). In many ways, such "tough-minded kinds," in one guise or another, were the exemplars of freedom in the 1960s. They did indeed stimulate each other's "creative elan" in the streets of Haight-Ashbury in San Francisco, at Monterey and Woodstock, even in their pastoral communes. It all ended—perhaps too soon. Some say it was because the movement lacked an ideology, lacked significant leadership to bring about political change. Others attribute it to the total separation from working-class organizations and unions (or to the hostility often aroused among workers with relatively conservative moral codes). Still others find the campus protests weakened by the rejection of black youth groups, who chose to conduct their own campaigns in the south. More than likely, the dissolution was due to the violence at Kent State and Jackson State, where real guns and real killings made symbolic violence and even symbolic peacemaking seem poignant, if not meaningless. Something was left, of course: the fragments of a Weather Underground; drug cults and sensitivity groups; a few "free schools" and intimate communities. Our questions, however, have to do with libertarianism as a position, with counterculturalism, and even with the human condition itself. When the Vietnam War ended (in defeat for the United States), when there seemed to be "no causes anymore," a kind of silence fell. The McGovern campaign seemed not only a failure but a death knell; the Watergate scandals seemed a mainstream, not a "New Left," cause; there was no more draft to defy. Perhaps most important of all, the main actors in the youth movement had left the campuses. Some had gone home again. Some found themselves in competition with the children of blue-collar workers for jobs. It would appear from our present vantage point that, except for women's groups and minorities and people traditionally oppressed, freedom was no longer a major issue for those who had been outraged, emptied of their faith.

As is well known, some of the values acted out on college campuses found another expression in what might be called educational "protest" literature. Writers like Edgar Z. Friedenberg, Paul Goodman, John Holt, George Dennison, James Herndon, and Herb Kohl won wide audiences with their sometimes Emersonian, sometimes socialist, sometimes humanist arguments against the institutional pressures of the public schools. The old myth, they said, was false. The schools could not and did not intend to "free" children from automatism or ignorance so that they could become participating citizens and, at once, pursue success. Rather, the schools were meant to impose certain value systems and constraints so that energies would be appropriately channeled to suit the requirements of the society. There was something basically at odds, it was said, between the demands of society and the requirements of human growth. Efforts should be made, in consequence, to provide spaces where children could be free *from* the culture's manipulations and pieties. Spontaneity should be encouraged, communalism sustained. In a certain respect, the sounds of Francis Parker's philosophy and of what Dewey called the "new" education were audible again. So was the Emersonian word that personal rebirth and regeneration provided the only sure ground for the development of a decent society. Imaginative as were some of the reforms proposed, sensitive as were some of the responses to children, they did not adequately deal with the old questions facing libertarianism. Is it sufficient to claim a negative freedom beyond the structures of society? What can such freedom signify without supports, without a public space? Are the primary obstacles to freedom to be found primarily in the structures of the institutions, in middle-class pieties, in artifices, in taboos? Are they found in a blindness to deficiencies in the world around us, in submergence in the everyday, in simple "thoughtlessness"? What do whatever answers we can find signify for those who teach?

When we consider the present moment, we need to take into account the transformation of what was once thought to be a beneficent social intelligence into "instrumental rationality" or what Jurgen Habermas has moved us to call action "governed by technical rules based on empirical knowledge" (1971, pp. 91–92). Our communication with one another, he tells us, has become distorted. Our talk is like technical or expert talk, "context free." The important decisions are made today apart from the domains of ordinary understandings, shared values, "consensual norms," and certainly apart from the language of daily life. Positivism, or a separating off of fact from value, dominates much of our thinking. Systems are posited that are to be regulated, not by what an articulate public may conceive to be worthwhile, but by calculable results, by tests of efficiency and effectiveness.

What has happened may be suggested by the difference between what Tom Joad saw as "drivin'" and oppressing him and what we presently try to visualize as an obstacle, or our particular "wall." For the Okies, it was the banks and the monstrous shapes of tractors levelling the fields. For student protesters three decades later, it was bureaucratic regulation, the misuse of knowledge, statistical controls. For us, the "wall" may also be found in increasingly faceless bureaucracies, in a "rule by Nobody" (Arendt, 1958), in the computerizations by which so much of our life is administered and controlled. It becomes more and more evident, in fact, that we inhabit an administered world, and that those who administer do so more often by mystifying messages than by containment or brute force. Behind us now are the memories of the entanglements of science with technology. There are memories, too, of the uses to which "freed intelligence" and human rationality can be put: surgical bombing, napalm production, counterinsurgency, "Star Wars," thought control. There remains the strain of identifying ourselves as fallible, questing human beings with respect to the computer networks, the simulations, the abstract models, the "games." Gleaming shapes of robots have in many places shoved aside the tractors that sent the Joad family on the road; but, today, for thousands of dislocated and obsolescent workers, migrant people, and jobless people, there is no place to go. Yet, from most points of view, they are free, are they not, as the managers of steel companies and farm equipment companies are free?

Seeking to clarify what that can mean, we may think back to Jefferson's connecting of freedom to action and dialogue within a public sphere. And we may recall Dewey's account of the "eclipse of the public" (1927/1954), surely a phenomenon even more significant now than it was 60 years ago. As we think back and try to think ahead, we may become sharply conscious of glass towers rising in cities, blocking out the burned-out buildings, the rusting infrastructures. We may abruptly perceive the strangers in the streets, hear the sounds of multiple dialects, feel the thrust and stasis of the crowds. We may picture the half-lit rooms and the passive faces before television sets, the flickering and persistent images, the incidental murmurings and messages. And we may feel the silences out in what ought to be, what may once have been, the public spaces, against the noise of motors and engines, the shrieks of sirens, the pounding of rock music, the thudding of wheels.

What is left for us then in this positivist, media-dominated, and self-centered time? How, with so much acquiescence and so much thoughtlessness around us, are we to open people to the power of possibility? How, given the emphasis on preparing the young for a society of high technology, are we to move them to perceive alternatives, to look at things as if they could be otherwise? And why? And to what ends?

Having taken the long, uneven journey from the days of Jefferson and the changing notions of freedom in what is still thought of as the New World, we have seen those who have taken advantage, those who have been stunned into helplessness, those who have defied suppression and repression, those who have turned in on themselves. We are now going to consider some of the predicaments and life stories of persons who could never take freedom for granted in this country: women, members of minority groups, immigrants, newcomers. We are going to look at how some of them, *naming* what stood in the way of their becoming, were able to posit openings in what appeared to most observers to be closed situations, openings through which they could move. We are going to engage with them, not from the vantage point of society or the system or the cosmos, but (wherever possible) from their vantage points as actors, agents in an unpredictable world. Freedom, we have seen, is the capacity to take initiatives, to begin. "It is in the nature of every new beginning," wrote Arendt, "that it breaks into the world as an 'infinite improbability,' yet it is precisely this infinitely improbable which actually constitutes the very texture of what we call real" (1961, p. 169). From the perspective of the system or the cosmos, things seem to

happen automatically, irresistibly. We think in terms of trends, prob-
abilities, statistical certainties. From a human perspective, that of a
teacher beginning a school year, a writer beginning a book, a child
beginning the first grade, nothing is fully predictable or determined.
All kinds of things are possible, although none can be guaranteed.
When risks are taken, when people do indeed act in their freedom, a
kind of miracle has taken place. Arendt reminds us that we ourselves
are the authors of such miracles, because it is we who perform
them—and we who have the capacity to establish a reality of our
own.

This is what we shall look for as we move: freedom developed by
human beings who have acted to make a space for themselves in the
presence of others, human beings become "challengers" ready for
alternatives, alternatives that include caring and community. And
we shall seek, as we go, implications for emancipatory education
conducted by and for those willing to take responsibility for themselves and for each other. We want to discover how to open spaces
for persons in their plurality, spaces where they can become different, where they can grow.

CHAPTER 3

Reaching from Private to Public: The Work of Women

The poet Muriel Rukeyser wrote:

> What would happen if one woman told the truth
> about her life?
> The world would split open.
>
> (1973, p. 377)

The lines are from a poem entitled "Käthe Kollwitz," dealing with the German artist known for her pictures of mothers and children, of people desecrated by famine and war. To tell the truth is to tear aside the conventional masks, the masks adopted due to convention or compliance, the masks that hide women's being in the world. It is to articulate a life story in a way that enables a woman to know perhaps for the first time how she has encountered the world and what she desires to do and be. Rukeyser's Kollwitz also says:

> I am in the world
> to change the world
> my lifetime
> is to love to endure to suffer the music
> to set its portrait
> up as a sheet of the world.
>
> (1973, p. 374)

To do that, for any woman to have done that, is to make question-able the categories that have contained feminine lives and, by so doing, to alter the other labels and categories that compose the taken-for-granted. If "the world" refers to interpreted experience or to commonsense constructs of what is taken to be real, it would indeed "split open" if people were to listen, to pay heed.

The first step, after all, is (to use Martin Heidegger's term) to "unconceal" (1971, p. 54 ff.). Concealment does not simply mean hiding; it means dissembling, presenting something as other than it is. To "unconceal" is to create clearings, spaces in the midst of things where decisions can be made. It is to break through the masked and the falsified, to reach toward what is also half-hidden or concealed. When a woman, when any human being, tries to tell the truth and act on it, there is no predicting what will happen. The "not yet" is always to a degree concealed. When one chooses to act on one's freedom, there are no guarantees.

A novel by Sue Miller, *The Good Mother* (1986), provides an example of this in the story of Anna Dunlop, recently and amicably divorced, who has been granted custody of her three-year-old daughter Molly. She loves Molly and enjoys her. Like many working mothers, she has to arrange day care for the child and baby-sitting; and there are moments when her obligations are a burden. Often guilty, trying to be as "good" as she knows how, she is burdened by the determinates of her own childhood. She had spent much time with her mother's patriarchal family and been indoctrinated with their conceptions of righteousness, duty, and success. Probably in consequence, she is in many ways cold, distanced from herself, convinced of her inadequacy, struggling for control. When she begins having an affair with an artist in Cambridge, she suddenly discovers all sorts of potentials in herself—for sexuality, for expres-siveness, for a free play of energies, for joy. She appears to gain a perspective on her own past and to transcend its determinacy, its weight. She has, on one occasion, been able to stand up to her stern and dominating grandfather and, in doing so, to enable her grand-mother to find her own voice in a grandchild's defense. But, through Anna's and her lover's carelessness, Molly has been exposed to too much of their intimacy; and the child communicates something to her own father that convinces him he should take her away from her mother. The misunderstanding brings on a court case, an argument about custody; and the child's father and his wife, representatives of the stable and conventional family, are awarded the little girl. Anna, given only visitation rights, thinks about Molly now being part of a

family and "the order, the deep pleasure in what happens predict-
ably, each day, the healing beauty of everything that is commonplace." She wishes she herself could be in a family again. "But that
isn't what I have, nor what I can offer Molly. I've made do with a
different set of circumstances—with our distance, our brief times
together, with all that's truncated, too little, too small in what we
have. And I take a certain pride in how well I've done this, in thinking
that perhaps I'm suited to it in some way, as other, more passionate
people might not be."

Surely, she is acceding to what she had been taught to take for
granted. She believed she had freely chosen the world Leo had
opened up to her, "where I was beautiful, and our sex together was
beautiful, and Molly was part of our love, our life." She was not
isolated or eccentric in her choosing; she had a group of friends
around her and Leo who lived by the norms of a more liberated life
than any she had known before. She may have been able to recognize the deceptions and manipulations in her family background; she
may even have realized the degree to which they expressed a patriarchal ideology. But she did not engage with them dialectically; she did
not explicitly identify them as obstacles to her fulfillment. What she
acknowledges as her lack of passion and her nagging wish for "the
healing beauty of everything that is commonplace" may be viewed as
a recognition that what she really wanted was to be as she was,
caught in the familiar and the acceptable. Or they may be viewed as a
sign of being hopelessly victimized by old myths of domesticity and
propriety, by a desire to please her grandfather first of all.

Anna Dunlop is legally free; her intelligence, as far as the reader
can tell, is not overly constrained by superstition or even mystification. She believes that the choices she is making and has made are
her own, that they can be accounted for by the activity of her own
mind. It might be said that she did not adequately rehearse in her
imagination the likely consequences of what she was doing and make
her decisions accordingly, with a proper understanding of the circumstances of her life. It might be said that her desires were incom-
patible or that she understood too little about her own dispositions.
What haunts the reader, however, is that talk of "all that's truncated,
too little, too small." The space of freedom has been narrowed
hopelessly. Refusing even the passion she had once discovered
through Leo, she closes off the power of possibility.

There is no question but that whatever freedom she could have
achieved would have been conditioned by obligation and relationship. (She *did* say that "Molly was part of our love, our life.") It may

or may not be the case that women, because of their early developmental histories, are more likely than men to make their moral decisions in a context of connectedness (Gilligan, 1982). It is certainly the case that, since the early days of the nineteenth century, women's efforts to reach out for their own freedom have been most often contextualized and concrete. With rare exceptions, they did not initially identify themselves as autonomous citizens and then stand up to demand their rights in what they thought of as a public sphere. They could not find their freedom on Walden ponds or on whaling voyages. Seldom could they establish themselves as managers or even property-owners. They did not even have control over their own bodies when it came to child-rearing or to illness of any kind. The truth about themselves, when revealed, had to do with what it meant to struggle against confinement and constriction, usually against what Virginia Woolf was to call "the cotton wool of daily life" (1939/1976, p. 72). They were unlikely to name their men as their oppressors, nor the inequitable system that deprived them of civil rights and equality of regard. It was, most often, the infinity of small tasks, the time-consuming obligations of housework and child care that narrowed the spaces in which they could choose.

The women who wrote in the nineteenth century tended to concentrate on daily life, therefore, on its details and textures, its ordinariness. Judith Fetterley writes that "it was not possible for these writers, or perhaps it was not of interest to them, to extrapolate from their own lives, their experience, and their perspective, and to see themselves as representative, universal, symbolic" (1985, p. 29). Nor did they ordinarily think in terms of an abstract totality. As they saw themselves, they were enmeshed and embedded in very specific ways. Their husbands, too, seemed to them to be equally enmeshed; few women writers pictured them striding alone on forest paths or creating worlds in noble solitude. For one thing, they knew how many women accompanied their husbands out west, how many went to sea, how many worked along with the men, even after the days of cottage industry. And they knew how strongly the men were drawn toward home from the factories and mines, and even from whaling voyages. From the female point of view, at least as rendered in letters and diaries, the dauntless and solitary hero of the myth did not exist. Indeed, the emergence of the so-called "domestic sphere" and the occasional "literary domestics" (Kelley, 1984) who managed to combine writing with their household tasks were all responsive to and in some sense created by husbands and fathers in need of refuge or of sanctuary.

Of course, there was love; there were, quite obviously, devotion and care. But there was something else, which Emily Dickinson captured, perhaps better than most, for all her seclusion and her single state:

> He put the belt around my life,—
> I heard the buckle snap.
> And turned away, imperial,
> My lifetime folding up.
> Deliberate, as a duke would do
> A kingdom's title-deed,—
> Henceforth a dedicated sort,
> A member of the cloud.
> Yet not too far to come at call,
> And do the little toils
> That make circuit of the rest,
> And deal occasional smiles
> To lives that stoop to notice mine
> And kindly ask it in,—
> Whose invitation, knew you not
> For whom I must decline?
> (1890/1959, pp. 85–86)

Some women, belted or not, succeeded in finding the hour or two a day they needed for writing. The daughter of one (a "good" wife) wrote about her mother, Elizabeth Stuart Phelps:

> She lived one of those rich and piteous lives such as only gifted women know: torn by the civil war of the dual nature which can be given to women only. . . . Now she sits correcting proof sheets, and now she is painting apostles for the baby's first Bible lesson. Now she is writing her new book, and now she is dyeing things canary-yellow in the white-oak dye—for the professor's salary is small, and a crushing economy was in those days one of the conditions of faculty life. . . . Now she is a popular writer, incredulous of her first success, with her future flashing before her; and now she is a tired, tender mother, crooning to a sick child, while the M.S. lies unprinted on the table, and the publishers are wishing their professor's wife was a free woman, childless and solitary, able to send copy as fast as it is wanted. The struggle killed her, but she fought until she fell. (Fetterley, 1985, p. 205)

In her book, *The Angel Over the Right Shoulder* (1852), Phelps imagines an angel writing down a story in which she is a character. The angel, she wrote, believed it important for her to cultivate her talents; but it was equally "right and important, to meet and perform faithfully all the little household cares and duties on which the comfort and virtue of her family depended; for into these things the angels carefully looked—and these duties and cares acquired a dignity from the strokes of that golden pen—they could not be neglected without danger" (Fetterley, 1985, p. 215). She could not, in the paltry few hours she carved out for herself, affirm herself to be an author—of her own text or of her life.

Rebecca Harding Davis (best and ironically known as the mother of Richard Harding Davis) wrote *Life in the Iron Mills* (1861) before she was married and never again attained that level of achievement. Tillie Olsen writes that that "was the price for children, home, love" (1978, p. 107). The book itself, written in Wheeling, West Virginia, and replete with images of iron bars, "slimy lives," "unsleeping engines," workmen's bodies governed by "the vast machinery of system," revealed to its readers the connection between social class and injustice, almost for the first time. Olsen believes it was made possible in part by the beginnings of the Women's Rights movement, by the publication of *Jane Eyre* and *Uncle Tom's Cabin*. Davis kept writing afterward, always asked to be more "cheerful," raging at slavery and the suppression of women, recognized neither during her life or at her death. Her work was so obliterated, says Olsen, that Eleanor Marx and Edward Aveling, whose *The Working Class Movement in America* appeared 30 years after *Life in the Iron Mills*, wrote that no American fiction writers had ever done "studies of factory-hands and of dwellers in tenement houses . . . pictures of those sunk in the inner depths of the modern *Inferno*" (Olsen, p. 112). Perhaps Davis said it best and most bitterly herself in a later short story: "Mother, here, will tell you a woman has no better work in life than the one she has taken up: to make herself a visible Providence to her husband and child."

Surely, they were caught—these "writing women"—in the mystification of the family. Carol Gould has written:

> The first mystification of woman as love goddess and madonna—in which even her natural functioning is spiritualized and glorified—is complemented by a second, equally pervasive mystification. Here the social and historical exploitation of women is hidden under the guise of its being her natural biological inheritance to bear and raise children, to be a housewife. This mystification seeks to keep woman in her place by making it her lot; it seeks to make her role acceptable by making it inevitable." (1976, p. 37)

It would appear that the capacity to understand this, to demystify it somehow, has something to do with human freedom, the power to choose and the power to act. It does not necessarily signify that the family, in and of itself, is an obstacle to freedom. It does suggest that the kind of social reality that demands such mystifications must be interrogated; the illusions must be exposed if women (and men as well) are to achieve the kind of freedom that will permit them to choose what they will become in whatever they decide will be their common world. Our history is filled with experiences (lost in what Tillie Olsen calls the "silences") of repression and self-destruction, of a terrible narrowing of energies that kept innumerable "free" people from creating their own humanity.

Kate Chopin's *The Awakening* dramatizes a dimension of this in the story of Edna Pontellier groping pathetically for her freedom in late-nineteenth-century Louisiana. The dreamy, fantasizing child of a patriarchal Presbyterian family, Edna marries a French Creole businessman, Leonce Pontellier, and they have two little boys. The early action of the novel takes place at a summer resort, Grand Isle, where Edna finds herself a stranger among the "mother-women" who, unlike herself, are devoted to their children and, at once, oddly outspoken, physical, and free. She tells one of them that she would give up her life for her children, but not herself; and, of course, she means that she wants a fulfillment greater than motherhood, although she is not sure what it is. Her husband is devoted to her and treats her like a helpless child; but she is experiencing a strange, unfamiliar "oppression, which seemed to generate in some unfamiliar part of her consciousness" (1972, p. 14). She does not blame him or lament at fate. "She was just having a good cry all to herself."

Her yearnings fasten on young Robert LeBrun, whose habit it is to flirt harmlessly with the women at the resort. He teaches her to overcome old fears and to swim; and she swims alone, reaching toward "the unlimited." Somehow, that new discovery makes her stand up to her husband for the first time when he asks her to come to bed.

> Another time she would have gone in at his request. She would, through habit, have yielded to his desire; not with any sense of submission or obedience to his compelling wishes, but unthinkingly, as we walk, move, sit, stand, go through the daily treadmill of the life which has been portioned out to us. (p. 52)

Like so many women of her time, she has let herself be victimized by what she has taken for granted "through habit" as natural, as given.

But her "awakening" is also an illusion. Fundamentally prudish, unable to confront her own sexuality, she confuses the stirrings within her with a desire to be a full person in the universe. Given the environment and her own rearing, however, she associates that with love for Robert, since she cannot imagine any real fulfillment without a male on whom she can depend. Assuming she (not a Creole) is committed to chastity, he runs off to Mexico, leaving her desolate. Home in New Orleans, however, she does identify alternatives for herself. She begins painting with some seriousness; she moves out of her husband's house; she even tramples on her wedding ring. Her husband, of course, assumes she is ill and consults a physician. She begins going out and having an affair with a man named Arobin, a pleasant rake who cannot satisfy her. When Robert returns and then leaves her again *because* (as he says) he loves her, when her friend tells her to "think of the children," she goes back to Grand Isle and to the beach. "Today it is Arobin; tomorrow it will be someone else." She begins swimming out to sea.

> There was no one thing in the world that she desired. There was no human being whom she wanted near her except Robert; and she even realized that the day would come when he would melt out of her existence, leaving her alone. The children appeared before her like antagonists who had overcome her, who had overpowered and sought to drive her into the soul's slavery for the rest of her days. (p. 189)

She drowns, remembering her father's home and her fantasies on the fields of bluegrass. All she has seen are two alternatives: to be a whore or a mother caught in "the soul's slavery." Caught between her own illusions and what she perceives as the arbitrary requirements of society, she has no choice. She cannot even summon up the possibility of a fully independent life without a man. She is legally free; she is wealthy; she is beautiful and talented; she has a family; and she dies. Nothing follows. The universe is unperturbed.

There were those, of course, like Catherine Beecher who realized that more dignity and more challenge were needed in the "domestic sphere" if people like Edna were to mature and survive. She believed that women, in many respects, chose their plight in the United States; and, for all their social subordination, they were given more consideration and respect than were women in any other country. At once, she recognized the "desultory and minute items" that preoccupied homemakers, how difficult it was to systematize housework in a changing society, how "inexperience and ignorance" along with poor health made many homemakers' lives unbearable (Hoffman, 1981, pp. 52–53). Beecher's remedy was appropriate education—in part to render homemaking more systematic and dignified, in part to increase the supply of competent domestic workers (who should, she thought, be working in homes rather than as operatives in factories), and to fill the ranks of teaching (the "noblest" profession) with unmarried women rather than men. For one thing, she believed that women's alternatives would be multiplied: They would not move so rapidly into marriage as their only option; and, if they did, they would at least be assured the kind of domestic help that would leave them to some extent "free." Surely it was important to enhance women's dignity and self-regard by rendering them, as it were, more effective practitioners; and it was important to attribute to their allotted "sphere" more worth and moral consequence than it was ordinarily given. But the question of whether or not this would contribute to their freedom remains a complex one, particularly since Catherine Beecher did not fundamentally question their subordination or their confinement to one "sphere." There is a respect in which this touches on the problem of whether any person can be free when enslaved. Freedom of mind and the opportunity to realize certain potentialities are conceivable under slavery. Within predetermined limits, enslaved persons have been known to believe they can exert their wills and achieve much of what they desire. It may even be that they can do so much of what they choose to do within these limits that they do not perceive them as obstacles. At what point does the existence of those limits provoke the vague sense of oppression experienced by an Edna Pontellier? In what sense do they give rise to the existential project engaged in by a Chopin or a Beecher? In what sense is a naming of those limits as obstacles required for the pursuit of freedom?

There are peculiar connections between some of the lived lives of American slaves in the nineteenth century and the lives of women at the time. Those called "house slaves" often lived relatively privileged lives. They were given important responsibilities, especially where the care of property and the rearing of children were concerned; numbers of them were educated. Certainly, in comparison with "field hands," they were granted (within the traditional limits) the power to act and the power to choose. Nonetheless, they were the ones most likely to strike out for their own and others' emancipation; they were the ones most likely to resist. This seems to have been most dramatically the case after 1830, when slavery was domesticated, meaning that it became "a domestic institution which came to mean slavery idealized, slavery translated into a fundamental and idealized institution, the family" (Rose, 1982, p. 21).

Slaves were treated as children in many places; they were different from the full human beings around them who happened to be white, in the sense that they presumably required more patriarchal "care" and control. This was so even when families were encouraged; fathers, mothers, and children (much like their white mistresses) were required to submit voluntarily to what was equivalent to parental control. Paula Giddings explains that women's resistance to slavery at the time was partly stimulated by their being used as sex objects by their masters, whose own wives—what with the ideal of chastity—were kept on pedestals. In a way like good and cherished daughters, black women were rewarded for their submission to the father figures; but, since they were not thought to be human in the way white women were human, their submission was expected to include acquiescence to seduction and sometimes to concubinage. Describing their internalized rebellion against this, Giddings writes that "the factor of reward . . . made this resistance a fundamentally feminist one, for at its base was a rejection of the notion that they were the master's property. So Black women had a double challenge under the new slavery: They had to resist the property relation (which was different in form, if not in nature, to that of White women) and they had to inculcate the same values into succeeding generations" (1984, p. 43). This meant, in many cases, a stern upbringing for their daughters, who had to be taught not to be seduced by favors, not to seek too much to please, not to let themselves be compromised. It was as if certain of the enslaved women were able to recognize what Nietzsche was to call a "slave morality" and to reject the Christian values of submissiveness and gratitude, often to save their own and their children's lives.

The stories of resistance by black women shed many kinds of light on the meanings of freedom and the search for freedom. This is, in part, because their struggles originated in what they personally lived and in the exploitation of their sexuality. As Catharine MacKinnon has said (1981), "Feminism fundamentally identifies sexuality as the primary social sphere of male power." In the case of female slaves, male power was that of the slaveowner-patriarch. Their efforts to achieve their freedom involved them in resistance to violations they shared with women in the same position and tried to articulate in stark and meaningful ways for the sake of their children. They knew, on some level, that it was their reproductive power even more than their labor power that was manipulated by their oppressors. The consequences of their being used by men masquerading as father figures were so devastating that they could not but find in the system itself the main obstacle to their growth as human beings. The ones who not only broke free but achieved freedom for themselves were the ones who took some kind of action against the system or its representatives—from poisoning their masters, to leading escapes on the Underground Railroad, to organizing anti-slavery societies when they arrived in the north. The Sartrean notion that freedom can be achieved only in a resistant world was played out in many female lives. Even today, in such writings as those of Maya Angelou, Alice Walker, Ntzake Shange, Toni Morrison, and Gloria Naylor, we find a dialectical relation to what surrounds us, a conscious pursuit of freedom as an existential project, a central life task.

The nineteenth-century narratives tell not only of humiliations and suffering. They tell of valiant efforts to be reunited with lost children and relatives. They tell of devious and protracted efforts, like Harriet Jacobs's years of hiding in a garret to avoid sexual harassment by her white master (Yellin, 1981, pp. 479–486), to find some kind of space where women could choose themselves as something other than objects or mere property. The news of what they suffered and what they achieved could not but arouse answering chords in white women attentive enough, and perhaps restive enough, to pay heed.

Sarah Grimké and her younger sister Angelina were the daughters of a South Carolina slaveholder; their own observations, coupled with a sense of shame, sent them off to the north and membership in the Society of Friends. Sarah Grimké's "Letters on the Equality of the Sexes" (1838/1972) explicitly links the "situation and degradation" of ordinary middle-class women to the plight of black women. Her writings expose male pressures on white women to be fashionable and "pretty toys" rather than thinking beings equal to men; and they challenge the narrow focus of female education on the domestic arts and the ways in which women are taught to view themselves as inferior. When the letters turn to "another class of women . . . to whom I cannot refer without feelings of the deepest shame and sorrow," they select out those issues that have to do with female sexuality. Grimké described slave markets where many black women were bought and sold "to gratify the brutal lust of those who bear the name of Christians," and wrote about the speculation in handsome young women, about the complicity of white women who accepted all that and turned away. Angelina Grimké, in her turn, took up the same cause even more eloquently. She went further to say that the "outrages of blood and nameless horror" were outright violations of the Bill of Rights and the Preamble to the Constitution.

Whether or not they were capable of an imaginative identification with black women, it is at least likely that the "shame" at what they suffered had something to do with their later involvement with the campaigns for women's rights. Granted, the plight of white women was masked and legitimated as that of black women would seldom be. Their "domestic sphere" was ascribed a moral luster that obscured the workings of male power; and they entered the anti-slavery arena with a conviction of moral agency. The Grimkés, like other women, experienced the humiliation of having to sit behind a curtain at abolitionist meetings. When Elizabeth Cady Stanton and Lucretia Mott attended an anti-slavery congress in London, they were outraged to find they could not be seated as delegates because they were women. A few years later, when Mrs. Stanton had moved to Seneca Falls, New York, and found herself overwhelmed with household tasks and family obligations, she experienced such discontent that she resolved to do something to remedy the "wrongs of society in general and women in particular." She went on:

> My experiences at the World Anti-Slavery Convention, all I had read of the legal status of women, and the oppression I saw everywhere, together swept across my soul, intensified now by many personal experiences. It seemed as if all the elements had conspired to impel me to some onward step. I could not see what to do or where to begin—my only thought was a public meeting for protest and discussion. (Flexner, 1975, pp. 73–74)

With the aid of Lucretia Mott, she organized the first of many conventions, the famous one at Seneca Falls in 1848.

They used the Declaration of Independence as a model for their Declaration of Principles:

> When in the course of human events, it becomes necessary for one portion of the family of man to assume among the people of the earth a position different from that they have hitherto occupied. . . .
> We hold these truths to be self-evident: that all men and women are created equal; that they are endowed by their Creator with certain inalienable rights: that among these are life, liberty, and the pursuit of happiness. (Schneir, 1972, p. 71)

At the end of the Declaration, there was a listing of the misunderstandings and attacks that had to be expected, along with plans for petitions, meetings, and publicity. Mrs. Stanton spoke to the assembled women of her own "sense of right and duty" and her conviction that only a woman could understand the degree of her "degradation." The long, usually unsuccessful campaign for women's suffrage in America is familiar by now, as is its involvement with the temperance movement and its separation from the anti-slavery movement on the issue of whether black men should be enfranchised before women. We know by now that Seneca Falls was only a stage in an ongoing struggle that, suffrage or no, is still incomplete.

What is of interest here is the significance of all this for an understanding of the problem of freedom. There are certainly echoes of the Jeffersonian view, not solely in the language of the Declaration itself, but in Mrs. Stanton's response to her own felt oppression with thought of "a public meeting for protest and discussion." Even if we assume that the public meetings and conventions opened spaces for groups of women to come together and experience a kind of freedom in the course of their encounters, we still have to acknowledge that women's experience cannot be defined in terms of abstract rights. We have to acknowledge as well that the language and the arguments devised by the campaigners for women's suffrage tended to be the language and arguments of liberal individualism. They were developed in the tradition of male autonomy and self-determination central to the "public sphere" males inhabited in contradistinction from the "private sphere." Now the women proponents of equal rights would seek independence from men in a realm apart from male domination or the "aristocracy of sex"; but they would call for its constitution in universalist, not particularist, terms. Even though Elizabeth Cady Stanton and others referred to their own "degradation," and even though many of the crusaders kept referring to the concrete circumstances that limited them and prevented them from spending sufficient time in the open with other campaigners for their rights, the implication was that "human" referred to something common and universal in both men and women. Overlooked was the long association of "human" with "rationality," for example, or with a capacity to conceive the Good in terms of universal principles rather than (as Kant said) in terms of "the pleasant as that which influences the will only by means of sensation from merely subjective causes" (1797/1949, p. 30). Because the public space was the arena where rational capacities could be realized, and where the Good could be given objective status, and because men were the actors in that space, it often followed that those excluded were considered less than human in the generic sense. Women, caught up as they were with intimate obligations and relationships, with intuitions and feelings, could not but be responsive to the sensed and the subjective.

Roberto Mangabeira Unger has written that the "estranged and the resigned share a common view of the relation of thought to life." And then:

> They both believe that there is a public realm of factual and technical discourse and an intimate world of feeling. Within the logic of private emotion all religion, art, and personal love is arrested, and from it all rational thought is banished. The narrow conception of reason as a faculty addressed to the public rather than to the private life, to means rather than ends, to facts rather than values, to form rather than to substance, is necessarily accompanied by the cult of an inward religiosity, aesthetic, and morality that thought cannot touch, nor language describe. (1975, p. 27)

It is conceivable that the campaigners for women's rights dichotomized their own experience when they chose to say so little in their public addresses about their families, their chores, their relationships in the concreteness of everyday life. Moreover, assigning the actualities of their lives to the domain of the wordless (except in personal letters written to one another), they were unable to confront the economic role of the family, the nature of their own exploitation (in their case, as unpaid labor), or the function of their mothering in reproducing (Chodorow, 1978) a certain kind of social organization. With all this in mind, it is difficult to conceive of them achieving their freedom or emancipation through the securing of political rights alone. It is similarly difficult to conceive of them achieving their freedom without integrating the private and public realms of discourse, without including "the world of feeling" in what they were constituting as an alternative public sphere.

A free act, after all, is a particularized one. It is undertaken from the standpoint of a particular, situated person trying to bring into existence something contingent on his/her hopes, expectations, and capacities. The world in which the person creates and works through a future project cannot but be a social world; and the nature of the project cannot but be affected by shared meanings and interpretations of existing social realities. John Dewey wrote, for example, that "while singular beings in their singularity think, want, and decide, *what* they think and strive for, the content of their beliefs and intentions is a subject matter provided by association" (1927/1954,

p. 25). If that association is conceived of as one among autonomous, rational beings who are convinced that reliable knowledge (being largely formal and rule-governed) does not vary among them, the very notion of singularity summons up a troubling relativism that makes suspect situated knowledge claims. This may partly explain, not only the lack of respect for women's thought processes on the part of men, but the efforts of certain women to suppress their own lived experiences in order to claim an equality in the domain of formal reason identified with the public sphere.

As Paul Ricoeur has said, however, autonomous acts of understanding are not the foundations of free choices; they are abstractions from concrete acts of stating, wishing, ordering, or deciding. What males have thought to be formal truths are grounded, in their cases as well as females', in the concreteness of experience and of encounters in the temporal world (Ricoeur, 1966, p. 43). In a *laissez-faire* society, however, where those in power relate to one another in contractual and conventional terms, where the private and the affective are excluded, the abstractions take on a pseudo-reality and an apparent objectivity. Women's concrete historical realities, on the other hand, are such that the particularities of everyday life are inescapable. They cannot simply claim their freedom and their rights (at least not ordinarily) and escape the sphere of obligation and concern. When they do so, they very often alienate themselves from what might be called the ground of their being.

To find an example of this, we need only look at the relationship between Susan B. Anthony, who never married and was forever on the road to campaign for women's rights, and Elizabeth Cady Stanton. Mrs. Stanton wrote many of the important speeches Anthony delivered; and, frequently, she was angrily accused of paying too much attention to her family activities. Stanton's letters constantly complain of the demands on her time at home. Once, she wrote to her friend: "As soon as you all begin to ask too much of me, I shall have a baby! Now, be careful, do not provoke me to that step!" (Tyler, 1944, p. 459). Male opponents kept reiterating that what such women were doing was not only infidel; it was opposed to "nature and the established order of society." When married women were asked to set aside their duties and to abandon the private sphere, they frequently (albeit secretly) may have felt the same. It follows that a "declaration of principles" or even a "declaration of independence" could not take the place of a critical confrontation with the actualities of the lived world if their freedom were to be achieved.

It may be that the antagonism aroused among women as well as men in the nineteenth century was partially due to the apparent forgetting of the concreteness of everyday life, the details of which were so present in women's literature. Indeed, this may often be the case in our own time. We hear more and more about modern feminists' neglect of the family, of working women's preoccupations, of the impacts of poverty on children. We are beginning to learn that, at least for women, freedom cannot be treated as an endowment. It does little good for a single mother, for instance, to assert her natural rights and her God-given liberties, if she cannot engage dialectically with the determining forces around her. Her life may be constricted and confined by the need to stay home most of the time due to a lack of day-care centers, by a functional illiteracy due to dropping out from school, by a lack of community and family support. The road to freedom for her can be opened only when she becomes aware of alternative possibilities for herself. It is true that she might abandon her children, take to drugs, become a prostitute when she finds her life to be unbearable. But these would be modes of escape, instances of negative freedom rather than resistance. It is unlikely that any of them would provide the kind of space she needs to decide what she wants to become in the world. If she were able to join with others who share a "common lot," and demand provision of day care so that they could go to work or return to school, if she were able to organize others to set up a storefront school in an empty building, she might find herself moving with those others toward a different life situation; she would herself become different; she would begin to grow.

Middle-class women at the end of the last century, like middle-class women now, seldom found examples or paradigms in such life stories, if they mentioned them at all. Ann Douglas writes of the "disestablishment" of numerous women who lost their practical functions in society with the decline of cottage industries and the rise of cities (1977). Many of them, working alongside equally debilitated liberal ministers, compensated by exerting "influence" through advertising, women's periodicals, in Victorian sentimentalism and religiosity. Doing so, says Douglas, they laid the foundations for modern mass culture and consumerism. A few "romantics" (such as Margaret Fuller and Herman Melville) defied sentimentalism and the incipient mass culture. "They had to try to move in straitjackets, and motion, not unpredictably, often became contortion—stunted, incomplete. Yet it was motion, and all the more significant because it took place under conditions and against odds that would increasingly prevail in America and elsewhere" (p. 256).

Generally hidden were the union girls in the Typographical Union, the women shoeworkers who formed the Daughters of St. Crispin, the women who joined the Knights of Labor (Wertheimer, 1977). Inaudible to the proponents of women's "influence" and most of the proponents of women's rights were such voices as those of the women unionists singing in Chicago:

> Shall song and music be forgot
>   When workers shall combine?
> With love united may they not
>   Have power almost divine?
> Shall idle drones still live like queens
>   On labor not their own?
> Shall women starve while thieves and rings
>   Reap where they have not sown?
>   (Wertheimer, 1977, p. 198)

They had to struggle against male opposition to their membership in unions, against the sweatshop economy that kept so many from starving, against a lack of education, against the constant threat of joblessness that afflicted them far more than it afflicted men. Even so, there were such women as Mary Kenney, the daughter of Irish immigrants, who organized women bookbinders into their own union, later conducted classes for young working women, founded the Women's Trade Union League, and later remained in Lawrence during the great textile strike to defy the American Federation of Labor and join the International Workers of the World. Stories like these, seldom told in the annals of American freedom, may well be exemplary for a time like ours.

Mary Kenney, it happened, won the support of Jane Addams, who was breaking her own trail toward the achievement of freedom at Hull House in Chicago. Like Lillian Wald and other early settlement house workers, Jane Addams moved from the language of Christian (and female) virtue to a language of social activism as she provided space and schooling to immigrant women, helped them form clubs and labor organizations, tried even to "humanize" labor by seeking to instill greater understanding of the workers' world and more sensitivity to what it meant to be members of a collectivity (Addams, 1902). Granting the tension between the desire to control and improve and the determination to set free, we can still see a convergence of Jane Addams's search for her own emancipation and the opportunities she helped open for newcomers to come together to emancipate themselves. In her case, too, it was not sufficient to declare and celebrate her freedom. She suffered the ordinary confinements as a girl; she sickened under their pressure; she went searching—through books, through travel, through friendships. She experienced what has been thought of as a conversion experience when she went to London and visited a mission called Toynbee Hall (Davis, 1973). It was a place that integrated religious ideas of the Social Gospel with Fabian and early socialist ideas; and it housed various young men from universities willing to live among and help the poor. Jane Addams not only resonated to its freedom from "professional doing good"; she found in it a solution for her personal dilemma: to commit herself to religious and domestic affairs *or* to social reform. Ellen Lagemann has laid out some of the difficulties confronting women like Jane Addams at the end of the nineteenth century. "The decision to establish a settlement ended Addams's despond. It brought into clearer focus all that she had learned at home, at Rockford, and in Europe. It helped her clarify her religious stand; and it enabled her to see a way in which she might combine her wish to be of service to others—a 'Breadgiver'—with her equally urgent wish to use and to gain influence—authority—through the powers of her mind" (1985, p. 17).

The long years of paralysis before that are indications of what could happen to women so long discouraged from using their minds and entering the public sphere. The medical profession was complicitous in suggesting repeatedly that too much rigorous thought, too much study would either weaken a woman's health or affect her reproductive organs; and Jane Addams had to deal with that as well. Her choice to establish Hull House and to move there with her associates is in many ways paradigmatic. Something in her situation (the visit to Toynbee Hall, notably) provoked her to see her own life differently, to posit alternative possibilities for herself. Friendships and alliances, especially with women like Ellen Gates Starr and (later) Julia Lathrop and Florence Kelley, helped give her the power to act on what she chose to do. There have been few cases where women so sharply defined the obstacles to their becoming, actually saw those obstacles as barriers to life itself.

Remarkable as well was the growing realization among the women developing Hull House and the many other settlement houses of the time that settlement work required more than an opening of middle-class culture to the neighborhood immigrants and poor people. Addams wrote of the reciprocity in the relationships developed with the neighborhood, and of the ways in which Hull House programs became responsive to neighborhood demands. What we find are expanding networks of connection and concern as her career in social work expanded. An instance of this can be found in one of Addams's treatments of what she saw as the "function of social settlement."

> A settlement in its attempt to apply the larger knowledge of life to industrial problems makes its appeal upon the assumption that the industrial problem is a social one, and the effort of a settlement in securing labor legislation is valuable largely in proportion as it can make both the working men and the rest of the community conscious of solidarity, and insists upon similarities rather than differences. A settlement constantly endeavors to make its neighborhood realize that it belongs to the city as a whole, and can only improve as the city improves. (Addams, 1899/1985, p. 93)

She spoke of repaving the streets, of a mass meeting to improve conditions in the factories, of a tracing of neighborhood murders to the recent Spanish-American War (and the war games played by children in the street), of alcoholism and the breakup of families due not only to moral failures but to the "sins of cupidity and failure to respond to social duty" on the part of the rich.

A book entitled *Women's Ways of Knowing* (Belenky et al., 1986) discusses the ways in which women's self-concepts and ways of knowing are intertwined, and how hard women often have to work to "claim the power of their own minds." What is particularly interesting about Jane Addams is the way in which she moved from her own lived world to an activist, relational stance in the wider world without losing touch with her ground. Each time she moved outward—past the settlement house door to the streets, to the factories, to the neighborhoods, to the city itself—she was enlarging the space for play of her own capacities, even as she was involving more and more people for the creation of some "in-between." The irony is that, in her role as social worker rather than sociological scholar, the things she and her colleagues came to know were not considered scholarly knowledge to be ranked with academic sociology. Social science was already becoming quantified; the preoccupation was with "objectivity" and "neutrality," values difficult to achieve or respect by the women involved with reciprocal relations with strangers, with the gaining of understanding, with action. As we have noted before, we may still have to confront the problems of gaining "truth" and reliable knowledge through multi-perspectival study, through interpretation. As has also been suggested, the idea of freedom, so long linked to self-direction and a separation of the subject from the objective world, may be revised and remade to the degree we understand situatedness and knowing in connection with action and speech, knowing as an aspect of vocation, taking place in the midst of life.

It is difficult to know how often Jane Addams and the other middle-class women in settlement house work actually thought of freedom as a value, although clearly much of what they accomplished led to the emancipation of other human beings. Their work cannot but evoke images of the committed "Yankee schoolmarms," who were not unlike them. They were the women, black and white, who went to hostile southern communities during and after the Civil War to teach the "freedmen" and their children (Hoffman, 1981, p. 91 ff.). One commentator wrote: "After making due allowance for all superficial enthusiasm and the romance which may be inseparable from the womanly nature and missionary labor, who can measure the significance of the fact that hundreds of young, gifted and cultivated women from the North are now scattered through the South as teachers of its former slaves?" (p. 109). The mystery of motivation remains in every case, as do the anachronisms of self-righteousness and "missionary" intent. What continues to be important, however, is the "singular" choices such women made. They were choices that moved them to take sometimes deadly risks in order to teach those desperately desiring to know—and, thereby, to achieve themselves.

We might say similar things about the openings achieved by middle-class women who did not take such risks, but who came together in networks and friendships to repair what they perceived as social lacks, and to bring about "reforms," often as volunteers (Lagemann, 1979). Largely because of the general preoccupation with negative freedom in American social history, such stories have not been viewed as accounts of people gaining—simply through their coming together—the power to act and the power to choose. Most women, as we have seen, remained confined by domestic duties, thrust into impotence by medical diagnoses, mystified by religiosity, submerged in what they were told was "natural" and altogether "right." There was, for some, the reminder that teaching was the only way for a woman to become mature and competent. Catherine Beecher, for instance, reminded her readers (especially her "well-educated, unmarried" readers, women of the wealthier classes) of the "suffering that results from the inactivity of cultivated intellect and feeling" (Hoffman, 1981, p. 49). Before taking on (or deprived of taking on) the "illustrious work" of motherhood, women ought to be sent, said Beecher, "to the most ignorant portions of our land, to raise up schools, to instruct in morals and piety, and to teach the domestic arts and virtues" (p. 51). For Nancy Hoffman, most teachers took on the responsibility because they needed work, or because their families were fearful of having spinsters on their hands. Now and then, a few admitted that they chose teaching because it offered independence when compared with marriage; and some others chose it explicitly to move the young "to collective action for temperance, for racial equality, for conversion to Christianity" (p. xviii).

What with the pressure on women to marry or to find some eminently virtuous substitute, it was desperately difficult for many to reach beyond toward a desired future. A kind of childishness often, a kind of innocence, made them vulnerable in unanticipated ways. Henry James, who left the country in part because of its narrowness and provincialism, its "bare little boxes of conventionality," discovered a metaphor in the ways in which the energies of young adolescent girls were deflected and constricted by the artifices of adult life. It was, for him, as if adults were threatened by the very existence of their young. The girls, in their turn, protected from knowledge of darkness, ambiguity, and complexity, were not allowed to test themselves against often dangerous actualities. In the context of our discussion, it might be said that that was how they were deprived of their freedom. They were not educated for a "resistant world."

James's *The Portrait of a Lady* can be viewed as a rendering of some of this, as it can be viewed as an "unconcealing" of the contradictions in the negative freedom so celebrated and prized in the American dream. Isabel Archer, in this novel, is wholly confident of her own independence as she is of her superiority; and she has "a fixed determination to regard the world as a place of brightness, of free expansion, of irresistible action" (1881/1979, p. 48). Believing she is not made for suffering, she is the very embodiment of innocent Americanism. Wholly convinced that she can control her own life, she refuses involvement for a long time with the assertion that she likes her own liberty too much. Taken to what she views as a rich and "romantic" England by her fiercely self-sufficient aunt, she is sucked into a culture whose pecuniary considerations she cannot see.

When her uncle leaves a fortune to her to enable her (as her cousin Ralph views it) to try out her wings, she is made vulnerable to the treacheries of those whose "defects" she is too blind and self-absorbed to see. Sure that she is protected against all outside interferences, she *looks* at everything from a distance, makes no judgments, does not (as is several times pointed out to her) "care." Before long, she is maneuvered into a marriage to an effete, amoral aesthete named Gilbert Osmond, a "collector" of objects, money, and human beings who can contribute to his status in some way. He imposes a "rigid system" on her; he treats her with contempt; at last, she realizes that "the real offence . . . was her having a mind of her own at all" (p. 398).

The point, though, is that she had made what appeared to be an entirely free and rational choice. Her actions, as far she knew, stemmed from herself. She had no consciousness of having been compelled. Moreover, at almost every juncture, she believed she could have chosen otherwise. Her friends not only tried to dissuade her from marrying Gilbert; they presented alternative possibilities. Her "reasons" were, in most respects, good reasons; they were even, to a large degree, principled. In Gilbert's "fine" Florentine ambience, she felt a certain "grossness" in her possession of so much money, spent only on herself. She thought the vulgarity of it could be overcome if she contributed it to a worthy cause; and Gilbert seemed a worthier cause than a hospital or a philanthropy. That was because he struck her as someone so splendid, gifted, and superior. In addition to that, her whole leisurely existence now seemed to her to be "devious, desultory"; there was no purpose in it. She was persuaded that it could be redeemed by Gilbert's love of "harmony, and order, and decency, and of the stately offices of life." In some way rootless, contextless, she saw herself becoming part of a fabric, a tradition. We might think back to the Hegelian idea (although, certainly, she did not) that a person can achieve an authentic freedom only by finding her allotted place in the cosmic order of things.

She did not realize that she had been caught in the "traps and treacheries" of a moneyed and stratified society until she suddenly became privy to Gilbert's intimacy with her admired friend Madame Merle—and recognized that she had been betrayed, actually "sold." Only then did she allow herself to name her predicament and acknowledge her unhappiness. Only then did she see that she had ushered herself, in felt autonomy, into "the house of darkness, the house of dumbness, the house of suffocation." She could not see what the reader is made to realize: that her own character and prejudices had helped create her vulnerability.

Her friend and would-be protector, the ostensibly liberated journalist Henrietta Stackpole, had tried to keep her in touch with Caspar Goodwood, a strong and presumably authentic American businessman, who obviously loves Isabel for herself. Henrietta has eyes of a "remarkable fixedness—which rested without impudence or defiance, but as if in conscientious exercise of a natural right, upon every object (they) happened to encounter" (p. 78). She boasts an unshakeable confidence in her own opinions; but she is what Isabel describes as "vulgar" and a "kind of emanation of the great democracy." Seeing her that way, Isabel gives evidence of an elitism not unlike Gilbert Osmond's. Her own inherent snobbery has made her susceptible to his view of the "stupidity, the depravity, the ignorance of mankind." She, too, seems to require a view of the "baseness and shabbiness" of other people's lives in order to feel superior. All this can be considered "causal" when it comes to the decisions she thought she was making in her freedom; but she had no way of understanding or critically confronting what she took for granted. Nor did she have any insight into the nature of the marketing society, of status hunger, of the economic aspects of the marriage institution, of ownership itself. As innocent with respect to the psychological as she was with respect to the social, she had no way of thinking about the role of her father in her upbringing, her relation to her married sisters, her own apparent sexual frigidity. Even at the end, when she decides to do the virtuous thing, to reject Caspar Goodwood one last time and return to her husband, she believes she is making an autonomous choice. She will do something for another human being now: She will try to save Gilbert's daughter Pansy from being "sold" as Isabel now thinks she was sold. She will compensate somehow for her own mistakes within the system, which (for her) remains a given and in most respects unchangeable.

In some sense we are back to *The Good Mother* and *The Awakening*. How much does the possibility of freedom depend on critical reflectiveness, on self-understanding, on insight into the world? How much does it depend on being with others in a caring relationship? How much depends on actually coming together with unknown others in a similar predicament, in an "existential project" reaching toward what is not yet? How much does it depend on an integration of the felt and the known, the subjective and the objective, the private and the public spheres? It must be clear enough that the mere assertion of freedom as a natural right or "independence" guarantees little when it comes to finding a space for personal becoming. This is so even though the rejection or ignoring of human rights (whether of women or slaves or oppressed people generally) can often destroy any possibility of choice. To overthrow tyranny or authoritarian controls, in other words, is not to bring freedom into being; it is only to allow for the search.

The search, however, never occurs in a vacuum. Freedom cannot be conceived apart from a matrix of social, economic, cultural, and psychological conditions. It is within the matrix that selves take shape or are created through choice of action in the changing situations of life. The degree and quality of whatever freedom is achieved are functions of the perspectives available, and of the reflectiveness on the choices made. But, as we have seen, the mystifications may be such as to distort the perspectives. What is taken to be reflectiveness or insight or foresight may—because of ignorance or fixation—lead to self-deception as in the case of Isabel. Or to suicide, as in Edna's case. Or to retreat into the "silences" Tillie Olsen has described.

Our interpretation depends, of course, on the vantage point taken. It is relevant to note that Henry James's was not a female vantage point. The narrative voice used in his novel is often ironic; it presents a view of the heroine as someone with an unbridled imagination, a "faculty of seeing without judging," and an "irreflective consciousness of many possessions." The picture is given an edge by the comment that Isabel has no sense of exclusion from the privileges of her world: "abundant opportunities for dancing, the latest publications, plenty of new dresses, the London *Spectator*, and a glimpse of contemporary aesthetics." And we are not sure whether the narrator is being critical of the "world" made accessible to middle-class girls or of Isabel herself. He goes on to explain that "the depths of this young lady's nature were in a very out-of-the-way place, between which and the surface communication was interrupted by a dozen capricious forces." She is unusual in being so eager and hungry for experience. She seems to be ennobled by the very reach of her imagination, by her glowing hopes, and even by the scope of her "delusions." The narrator appears to love her even as he points out the ways in which she has been spoiled by indulgence and overprotection, corrupted by her felt superiority. For all that, the implication is that the "lady's" own innocence and deficiencies are to be blamed for what happened. A properly educated individual, one able to judge and to care and to see through the artifices of convention, would have been able to avoid the traps.

The fictional worlds created by women like Edith Wharton and, say, Harriette Arnow differ considerably from James's. In Wharton's case, the weight of determining forces is made to appear too heavy to resist, no matter what the degree of insight or understanding. In *The House of Mirth*, Lily Bart is intelligent enough, although her mind "shrank from the glare of thought." She sees entry into the garish, intriguing world of wealth as her only way of escaping poverty and surviving as a person. Her view is not unusual, given her social class and rearing, and the predicament of being the daughter of a rich man who had been ruined. She believes that, through careful design, she can maneuver the "crowded and selfish world of pleasure," find a wealthy husband, and remain who she is. There are times, of course, when she feels two beings within her, "one drawing deep breaths of freedom and exhilaration, the other gasping for air in a little black prison of fears" (1905/1964, p. 69). She realizes the pretenses, the sophistries, the humiliations that will be asked of her if she "makes it" in the social world; but she says that freedom is an "indulgence" for someone like her. She has, she thinks, to acquiesce to a life she despises for the sake of her security. At length, she is cast out of that life when she tries to cling to some kind of moral code. What was once taken for granted as the natural order of things suddenly begins to seem a chaos. The men and women leading their ritualized, pleasure-seeking lives now strike her as "atoms whirling away from each other in some wild centrifugal dance"; she finds herself lost and alone on the rainy, inhospitable streets of New York.

> She had learned by experience that she had neither the aptitude nor the constancy to remake her life on new lines, to become a worker among workers and let the world of luxury and pleasure sweep by her unregarded. She could not hold herself much to blame for this ineffectiveness, and she was perhaps less to blame than she believed. Inherited tendencies had combined with early training to make her the highly specialized product she was: an organism as helpless out of its narrow range as the sea-anemone torn from the rock. (p. 311)

There is no sustaining community within her sight or grasp. She is given one belated glimpse of continuity when she holds Nellie Struthers's baby for a moment and feels, for an instant, the "old life-hunger." Soon, dreaming she has the child in her arms, she unintentionally takes an overdose of sleeping pills. She is not fully responsible for her own death.

As in the case of other naturalistic renderings at the time, the view is deterministic, far more pessimistic than Henry James's. Isabel is made to seem responsible for what she does, while Lily Bart cannot be "blamed" because she is so helpless against the forces buffeting her within and without. Neither one, however, considers the possibility of an alternative social order; and neither makes any effort to come together with others in order to transform, or to find openings, or to resist. Today, looking back from a time when women have won general acceptance for being workers "among workers," we can appreciate the stringency of the traditional dichotomies and the ways in which acceptance of them eroded women's capacities. A novel like *The House of Mirth* may be read as exposure, challenge, or critique. It may appeal to the indignation, even the freedom, of the reader. It may move some readers, in their restlessness, to affirm that women like Lily Bart have to be held responsible. As human beings, they are obligated to resist.

When we turn to Arnow's *The Dollmaker*, written nearly half a century later, our indignation is likely to focus on the evils and the inequities of the economic system, not the deficiencies of the mountain woman Gertie Nevels. In her home environment, she is powerful and courageous, capable even of resisting uniformed authority to save the life of a child. When her husband gets a war-time factory job in Detroit, she is compelled to join him with her children and give up her plans for buying her own home in Kentucky. The compulsion stems from her mother's reminder of St. Paul's dictum that a wife must follow her husband, and from her own guilt at what she has been made to think of as unwomanliness. Once in Detroit, she falls victim to the confinements and demands of urban poverty. She has to abandon her own self-expression, whittling beautiful dolls out of wood. Economic necessity forces her to use her talent in jigsaw production of identical Christ figures. The requirements of "adjustment" force her to deprive her disabled little daughter of her imaginary playmate, Callie Lou; and the child, pursuing her playmate, is run down by a locomotive, a fearsome metaphor for what oppresses, destroys, and overwhelms. All but one of the other children adapt to the devices and the consumerism of proletarian America, as strikes are broken, and people are cheated and offered false promises. Gertie finally splinters the wood she has been saving, half-sculpted, with the face of Christ half-hidden; there is no going home again.

We are presented with a picture in which ideology and alienation interlock. The world created is one in which trade unions are insufficient, workers are divided against one another, the young are socialized into "needing" more and more consumer goods. In some respect, freedom here is associated with the rural past and the mountain community the Nevels family has left behind. It is identified with self-determination, even private ownership (and planting and whittling) in a disappearing world. At once, given the necessities inherent in the capitalist system itself, freedom appears to signify the negation of what exploits workers, hurts children, or presses down on people in their helplessness. The only voice suggesting radical change is that of a middle-class intellectual. Whatever collectivity might exist is still potential, like the Christ face not yet carved out of the wood.

We are left in incompleteness, especially if we hold in mind the situatedness that has so much to do with becoming human and with the power to choose. What would happen, what would have happened if the Nevels family had joined a revolutionary group committed to expropriation of the owning class? What would have happened if the racial and ethnic prejudices among the poor people of Detroit had been removed? What would have happened if the poor had come to accept a doctrine or a formula for bringing about structural change? Would it have made a difference to little children who yearned after imaginary playmates, who could not "adjust" to their schools? Would it release Gertie Nevels for "useless" doll-making? Would it enable her and the other women on the street to break, if they chose, with the demands of domesticity and find some alternative to their everyday lives?

Surely, it would have made a difference if they came to realize that what they took for granted as "natural" and inexorable was a human construction, susceptible to reinterpretation and change. It would have made a difference if they could reconstitute their own internalized visions of themselves. We are back to the dialectic, back to the subject/object relationship and the realization that freedom can be achieved only in an ongoing transaction, one that is visible and legible to those involved. Yes, as women have learned in recent times, there must be structural and systemic changes: Employment opportunities must open; options must be expanded; support systems must be strengthened to keep families viable and secure. Women will continue to affirm their rights to self-determination and equal treatment in the schools and marketplaces of the nation; they will continue, in various domains, to seek positions of leadership and power, even if that means becoming as competitive and self-directing as men. And, indeed, it appears that, for many women today, the quest for freedom remains a quest for something too long denied. Sharply aware of the ways in which male identity seems to depend on traditional gender separations, such women struggle against the subordination this always seems to impose. If they do so alone, without experiences of friendship and sisterhood, they are likely to feel abandoned, existing in a void. Certain novels come to mind: Joan Didion's *Play It As It Lays* (1970); Alice McDermott's *That Night* (1987). In both cases, women feel abandoned because they have lost their fathers. The substitutions they seek are always in some sense illusory or unsatisfying. Sometimes, as in Toni Morrison's *Sula*, they see themselves "going down like one of those redwoods," claiming that they "sure did live in this world" (1975, p. 123). Sula is a black woman, of course, living in a place with few external supports, a world of which she cannot make coherent sense. When asked what she has to show for her autonomy when she is dying, she says, "'Girl, I got my mind. And what goes on in it. Which is to say, I got me.'" Her friend asks, "'Lonely, ain't it?' 'Yes. But my lonely is *mine*.'" She has been a kind of pariah in her town; and her self-dependence is in many ways due to the fragmentation and eventual collapse of an exploited community, of what had, once at least, been a "place." But she may become a kind of metaphor for other "free" women in our world today: office executives striving for control; single mothers living alone with their children; rootless women, traveling women living in the "lightness of being"; academic women scholars intent on intellectual purity.

In any case, the terms of the dialogue regarding women have changed to a large degree. The crucial development in inquiry about women's lives and possibilities has had to do with the probing of the distinctiveness in women's moral development, ethics, and modes of knowing. Carol Gilligan's *In a Different Voice* (1981) works within the framework of cognitive psychology and challenges the point of view that emphasizes autonomy as the highest stage of moral development, and principled decision making as superior to bonds of human affection. Because women have different kinds of experience when growing up, writes Gilligan, their values differ as do their moralities. Indeed, she speaks of choices being made in a fabric of mutuality and concern, of ongoing dialogue and conversation, of cooperation rather than competition, of play rather than rule-governed games. Rather than focusing on their rights in human encounters, she says, women are more prone to think in terms of responsibility. In Nel Noddings's *Caring* (1984), a philosophical approach to feminine ethics and moral education, the ethical ideal has to do with caring and being cared for. "Caring," Noddings writes, "preserves both the group and the individual and . . . limits our obligation so that it may be realistically met. It will not allow us to be distracted by visions of universal love, perfect justice, or a world unified under principle" (p. 101). Important ethical choices are not made according to rational principle. They depend on "the will to be good, to remain in caring relation to the other."

It is relevant to our concern that neither Noddings nor Gilligan deals with the conception of freedom. Freedom, as concept or condition, is not listed in the index of either of their books; nor is it in the various studies of women's distinctive "ways of knowing," including those dealing with the connection between gender and scientific research (Keller, 1985), gender and relational thinking, or "mothering" approaches to the world. Strangely or not, it appears that freedom in its negative sense was of such overriding importance in women's lives that few people thought of what it might signify in another sense, once the constraints of the "feminine mystique," outright job discrimination, and marital domination were released. We need only recall the Rukeyser verse with which we began: "I am in the world to change the world."

Mutuality and concern (if, indeed, they characterize most women's lives) are not in themselves enough to change the world; nor is the affirmation of responsibility for others. Some believe it is at first necessary to replace language that denies body and feeling, as does the still dominant male discourse, with a new female expressiveness. Female imagery should be used even to describe and explain public and cultural conditions in terms of personal experience. Mary Daly, for instance, following Gertrude Stein's linguistic lead, writes about breaking through male deceptions with an act of dispossession that is "absolutely Anti-androcrat. A-mazingly Anti-male, Furiously and Finally Female" (1978, p. 29). She ends her book with talk about hearing and spinning, spinning what we hear. "We can weave and unweave," she says, "knot and unknot, only because we hear, what we hear, and as well as we hear. Spinning is celebration/cerebration. Spinsters Spin all ways, always. Gyn/Ecology is UnCreation. Gyn/Ecology is Creation" (p. 424). This may be, certain feminists believe, the only way of breaking with the supposedly universal patriarchal point of view. Others, like Julie Kristeva, remind them that going beyond language and culture in this fashion can lead to hysteria, if not to the contempt of those who try to read (1975).

It may be possible to hold in mind and to make audible the fragile aspects of human existence, even as it may be necessary to point over and over to the centrality of bonding and caring and touching while allowing for the articulation of the multiple perspectives we have spoken of above. Clifford Geertz writes about the "animating paradox" in the recognition that "thought is spectacularly multiple as product and wondrously singular as process" (1983, p. 215). Terry Eagleton points out the ways in which the women's movement has put "identity and relationship centrally at stake, renewing attention to lived experience and the discourse of the body" and made them politically relevant (1983, p. 215). They can, it would appear, become politically relevant only if they can contribute to the creation of the public space.

We might recall once again Hannah Arendt's rendering of René Char's Resistance story: how he and his comrades had become "challengers" and begun creating "that public space between themselves where freedom could appear" (1961, p. 4). He says at the end: "At every meal that we eat together, freedom is invited to sit down. The chair remains vacant, but the place is set." Perhaps we can relate the conceptions of caring and concern to the setting of such a table, the creating of that space. It remains a matter, for men and women both, to establish a place for freedom in the world of the given—and to do so in concern and with care, so that what is indecent can be transformed and what is unendurable may be overcome.

CHAPTER 4

Multiplicities, Pluralities, and a Common World

We have been speaking of multiple perspectives, thinking about freedom in relation to community and to the possibility of a common world. We cannot think about American education without summoning up images of newcomers, of strangers. There have always been children from immigrant families, children who are "different" but who must still be initiated into what we conceive to be our way of life. There are always strangers, people with their own cultural memories, with voices aching to be heard. They have always been coming; they are still coming from the ravaged places, the police states, the camps, the war-torn streets. Some come for sanctuary; some, for opportunity; some, for freedom. What they understand to be freedom depends on their traditions and their life experiences, their hopes, often their dreams.

The blacks were among the first to come; and their experience has been in painful ways unique, because most did not choose to come to this country; and they came deprived of their freedom. Nevertheless, their music, their poetry, their articulations have given expression to the archetypal predicament of the outsider more eloquently than have those of many others. This may be because, once we began paying heed to them, we found them speaking from the heart of American culture and through the learned idioms of its longings. They were unable to gather around themselves the memories, rituals, and traditions of abandoned homes or homelands as others could, because they were torn apart from those who had shared their lives. They had continually to create and recreate their own traditions out of the languages available in this country, the sermons, the hymns, the prescriptions, the prayers; and they did so in the constant awareness of exclusion, humiliation, and threat. Knowing the underside of the nation's dream of freedom, they often put into words or sounds what lay at the core of other people's emancipatory visions. Here, for example, is Langston Hughes:

> It was a long time ago.
> I have almost forgotten my dream.
> But it was there then,
> In front of me,
> Bright as a sun—
> My dream.
>
> And then the wall rose,
> Rose slowly,
> Slowly,
> Between me and my dream.
> Rose slowly, slowly,
> Dimming,
> Hiding,
> The light of my dream.
> Rose until it touched the sky—
> The wall.
>
> (1968, p. 426)

We may find that the search for freedom, in personal and shared lives, almost inevitably led to an engagement with that wall. We may think of the Irish in the days of the "great hunger" before the Civil War, living in shanties and tenements on the edges of New York and Boston, fighting prejudices against "Paddy," taking the menial jobs. We may think of Scandinavians fleeing orthodoxies and something resembling serfdom, making their way to the midwest to what were for years empty and rugged places, where they struggled to survive. We may think of the Jews in the ghetto sweatshops, in small un- heated rooms, laboring to keep their families together, their time- worn practices alive. And we may recall the blacks, escaping in the slave years through the Underground Railroad, shipped northward in trucks later on to work that may or may not have awaited them, suffering discrimination all the way, challenging, forever challenging "the wall." We who are in education cannot know, cannot truly know how it was, how it is. But we can attend to some of the voices, some of the stories. And, as we do so, our perspectives on the meanings of freedom and the possibility of freedom in this country may particularize and expand.

It is, in some degree, an astonishing experience to consider what Frederick Douglass achieved in the search for freedom. We can recall the tales of his abysmal suffering as a slave—beaten, moved about, humiliated, jailed. While still young, he managed to run away and to survive through his own efforts in cities in the north. What was remarkable was his insatiability when it came to the pursuit of freedom, and not only for himself. He campaigned for free and equal education, for women's rights, for abolition, for Irish home rule here and abroad. We know from his autobiography (1855) the risks he took in his refusal to accept merely negative freedom; we are familiar, also, with his belief that freedom could be won only by continuing resistance. In 1857, he said:

> The whole history of the progress of human liberty shows that all concessions yet made to her august claims, have been born of earnest struggle. The conflict has been exciting, agitating, all-absorbing, and, for the time being, putting all other tumults into silence. If there is no struggle there is no progress. Those who profess to favor freedom and yet deprecate agitation, are men who want crops without plowing up the ground, they want rain without thunder and lightning. They want the ocean without the awful roar of its many waters. (1857/1967, pp. 21–22)

Submission, he said, intensifies injustice. Endurance strengthens tyranny. Like Harriet Tubman, who kept returning to the south to free other slaves after she herself was free, Douglass believed that freedom demanded the taking of constant initiatives along with others. His own emancipation meant provoking the oppressed in other places to take resistant action, to assert their own claims for equal treatment and respect for their rights.

Granted, Douglass and Tubman had experienced slavery, which must be viewed as the ultimate oppression. Granted, too, he could never have felt the environment to be wholly sympathetic, wherever he was. His autobiography indicates that there were always feelings of compulsion, always a sense of being labelled or objectified. Neither before nor after the Civil War could he feel anything resembling the "lightness" of which Kundera writes. Nor, when he was no longer a slave, could he feel himself to be walking spontaneously through his life. At once, like other human beings, he must often have had the feeling that he was what he was, that the skills and habits he had already acquired fixed him in place somehow and made him predictable even to himself. That is why he may be considered in some respect exemplary: He continued to find new meanings in his lived situations. Relating to women or to Irish rebels or to President Harrison (whom he futilely asked to condemn lynching in his annual address to Congress) or to other abolitionists in the north, he continued to endow his world with different meanings, to question the significance it already seemed to possess. This is one way of conceiving of what freedom signifies—the freedom to alter situations by reinterpreting them and, by so doing, seeing oneself as a person in a new perspective. Once that happens, there are new beginnings, new actions to undertake in the world.

Certain of the early abolitionists had similar experiences, especially when they saw themselves in startling new relationships with black people, relationships that made them challenge customary views of what it meant to be Christian or American or a middle-class intellectual taking it for granted that he/she was free. As James McPherson has pointed out, however, it was difficult for many of them to hold to their views of resistance and emancipation after the Civil War and the Reconstruction period in the south. Impressed, as numerous thinkers were, by the discovery of evolution, they began applying Darwinian concepts to the problem of racial progress. Numbers of them began speaking in terms of gradualism and the need to depend on natural forces rather than human action or struggle to bring about the desired changes. Abram Stephens was more or less representative when he said that social change "that is hastened or brought about by violent means is, as far as true progress is concerned, a *stumble*, not a step. It may be questioned if even the anti-slavery reform were not at last consummated too precipitately; if a more gradual emancipation, including a preparatory education for freedom, might not have been better" (McPherson, 1968, p. 138). In the face of terrible lynchings, poll taxes, Jim Crow laws and the rest, one well-meaning reformer after the other called for time and patience, "the harmonizing and healing effects of time." We might be reminded of Ike McCaslin in William Faulkner's *The Bear* (1942/1958) praising the "virtues" of black people: endurance "and pity and tolerance and forbearance and fidelity and love of children" (p. 282). In effect, he was calling on them to be patient, to be true to their own morality. When a young man comes to him and insists that, once freed, the blacks should be given a place in the New

Canaan, old McCaslin tries to tell him that they will be cheated anyway and plunged into poverty. And the old man keeps insisting: "They will endure."

The welcoming applause Booker T. Washington received in 1895, in Atlanta, is not surprising, when we consider the ways in which what he called "the great leap from slavery to freedom" was being conceived. He said there was a danger of forgetting that the masses had to live by the work of their hands. Released slaves should recognize that "the agitation of questions of social equality" was a folly, and that the blacks had to be "prepared" for the privileges they were being offered. He told his audience not to

> fail to keep in mind that we shall prosper in proportion as we learn to dignify and glorify common labor and put brains and skill into the common occupations of life; shall prosper in proportion as we learn to draw the line between the superficial and the substantial, the ornamental gewgaws of life and the useful. No race can prosper till it learns that there is as much dignity in tilling a field as in writing a poem. It is at the bottom of life we must begin, and not at the top. Nor should we permit our grievances to overshadow our opportunities. (1901)

Read from the contemporary point of view, Washington appears to have been institutionalizing an "Uncle Tom" image by calling for friendly relations with the white man while remaining socially separate "like the fingers of a hand." We may be aware of the challenge to him posed by W. E. B. DuBois, who objected to Washington's proposals for industrial schools for black men. He wrote:

> Is life not more than meat, and the body more than raiment? And men ask this today all the more eagerly because of sinister signs in recent educational movements. The tendency is here, born of slavery and quickened to renewed life by the crazy imperialism of the day, to regard human beings as among the material resources of a land to be trained with an eye single to future dividends. Race-prejudices, which keep brown and black men in their "places," we are coming to regard as useful allies with such a theory, no matter how much they may dull the ambition and sicken the hearts of struggling human beings." (1903/ 1982, p. 126)

In fact, DuBois believed that "questions of social equality" should be dealt with directly and that "Negroes must insist continually, in season and out of season, that voting is necessary to proper manhood, that color discrimination is barbarism" (p. 87 ff.).

For all that, the issue raised by Washington has been a real one in the history of freedom in the United States, and particularly freedom in relation to education. In many respects, he was in the tradition of Horace Mann and the other spokesmen for common school reform. Not only did people have to be prepared to live in freedom, they believed; it was education and not political action that would, as time went on, open opportunities for the long deprived, secure the social order, and make for a more productive society. We have already seen the impacts of what has been called "social Darwinism" on educational thinking at the start of this century, as we have seen personal freedom linked to appropriate participation in the institutional order of things. By now we are painfully aware of the slow pace of black "prospering" in both south and north. We have found that freedom is hardly likely to be achieved simply through the opening of opportunities. Some kind of reciprocity is required between individuals in quest of freedom and the persons surrounding them; and it seems evident that common schooling was not sufficient. It was, for too many years, in no way "common," particularly in the south; it was not "equal," even in the north; it did not, *qua* institution, empower the young to reach beyond themselves.

In *The Souls of Black Folk,* Dr. DuBois wrote with prescience about the weakness of the common school system where blacks were concerned (1903/1982, p. 120 ff.), in a segregated situation where schooling generally meant "training" before the "gate of toil." He wrote of the long-standing shortage of teachers, particularly black teachers. With special eloquence, he called for college and university education for the "talented." (He, after all, had achieved a Harvard graduate degree.) "We shall hardly induce black men to believe that if their stomachs be full, it matters little about their brains. They already dimly perceive that the paths of peace winding between honest toil and dignified manhood call for the guidance of skillful thinkers, the loving, reverent comradeship between the black lowly and the black men emancipated by training and culture" (p. 138). Once more black men found expression, he said, once more of them were enabled to seek "a freedom for expansion and self-development," the world at large would be given new points of view.

There is something peculiarly significant about this recognition of continuity between the strivings of a suffering group and the opening of the spaces inhabited by the majority. Those spaces, those lived situations could not but be constricted by one-dimensional and racist thinking. The perspectives of choice itself could not but be narrowed and warped. Blacks, said DuBois in "Strivings of the Negro

People," (1897, 1970, p. 25) needed to seek work, culture, and liberty together. In time, these ideals would coalesce; and a higher meaning would be found in the very fostering of black people's "traits and talents." And some day "on American soil, two world races may give each to each other characteristics which both so badly lack."

Fifty years later, when asked about the "color line," DuBois said it was the century's problem. Now he associated it with the fact that so many people were willing to live in comfort at the price of "poverty, ignorance, and disease" among the majority of their fellow men. Can freedom be authentic if it is pursued at the cost of others' freedom, others' welfare? For Gunnar Myrdal, writing *An American Dilemma* (1962), the "Negro problem" was a moral issue and the "White man's problem." If, as he put it, the American Creed represents the national conscience, the "Negro problem" is a problem because "of a palpable conflict between the status actually awarded him and those ideals" (p. 23).

In this context, prejudice against the American Negro is comparable to the anti-Semitism Jean Paul Sartre described (1948) and related to American bigotry. For Sartre, anti-Semitism was not a Jewish problem any more than the Negro problem was a problem for blacks. Anti-Semitism was a problem for all the French who were not Jews. He believed that they were the ones who ought to form a league against all sorts of anti-Semitism, a "concrete community engaged in a particular fight" characterized by at least some of the passion anti-Semites muster when they are attacking Jews. "In order to awaken this passion, what is needed is not an appeal to the generosity of the Aryans. . . . What must be done is to point out to each one that the fate of the Jews is *his* fate. Not one Frenchman will be free so long as the Jews do not enjoy the fullness of their rights. Not one Frenchman can be secure so long as a single Jew—in France or in the world at large—can fear for his life" (1948, p. 153). This was written some years after the war and the discovery of the Final Solution; and it may be an account of what Sartre had learned about the insufficiencies of education, interdiction, even law where anti-Semitism was concerned. The difficulty with education, useful as it might be, he said, was that it might have only an individual reference. Laws would never embarrass an anti-Semite, because he saw the society to which he belonged as existing beyond the bounds of legality. It was a phenomenon of a society where human beings were separated from one another, where the members did not feel "mutual bonds of solidarity" as they would if they were all engaged in "the same enterprise" (p. 150). I think this applies to prejudice against black people in this country as well, as I think Dr. DuBois believed in his own terms and in his own time. It is entirely likely as well that people demean and turn against black people (as they have toward the Jews) because of the ways in which they "read" or interpret their situations. For Sartre, it was a matter of changing "the perspective of choice" (no matter how that choice was derived), not attacking the freedom of the bigot. "We do not attack freedom, but bring it about that freedom decides on other bases, and in terms of other structures."

It probably took until the 1960s and the Civil Rights movement before freedom, among signal groups of Americans, began making choices on other bases. We know about the long tolerance for Jim Crow and the Ku Klux Klan in the south; we know about the broken dreams up north. Less is known with respect to the fearful predicaments of black women, even the strong and matriarchal women who maintained their families and did what was required to help them survive. They experienced abandonment and humiliation from the men in their own lives; they, too often, felt themselves treated as "quarry," even as they were oppressed by the outside world, including the women for whom they worked. Paula Giddings quotes Anne Julia Cooper saying, in 1892, that it was not so much a question of women asking how they should "so cramp, stunt, and simplify, and nullify" themselves to become eligible for "the honor of being swallowed up" by little men. Rather, it was a male problem having to do with how the man could so develop as "to reach the ideal of a generation of women who demand the noblest, grandest, and best achievements of which he was capable" (1984, p. 113). Nonetheless, for many it was impossible to fulfill themselves without the good fortune of being allied to a moderately successful man. It was, clearly, a matter of greater suffering to be a woman alone and with children, to be a slave or a laundress or a factory worker—and to manage to be strong, to support others, to stay alive.

In addition to the nameless ones and the invisible ones—maintaining families, teaching in schools, organizing unions, doing pastoral duty, singing in choruses—there were artists in the Harlem Renaissance reaching out for their freedom, attaining the freedom of poetry and of the novel and sometimes of the play. Whether it was Jean Toomer recovering something of his own past in *Cane*, Countee Cullen tapping a Keatsian passion and musing on Africa, or Langston Hughes saying it as "truly" as any poet could about life in the ghetto and a "dream deferred"—they were yearning beyond objectness. They were discovering their voices and at once reaching toward membership in a tradition. And always, always, there was the strain that the singular voice could not allay, the memory nothing could still. Sterling Brown wrote (in response to a line by Carl Sandburg):

> They dragged you from homeland,
> They chained you in coffles,
> They huddled you in spoon-fashion in filthy hatches.
> They sold you to give a few gentlemen ease.
> They broke you in like oxen,
> They scourged you,
> They branded you,
> They made your women breeders,
> They swelled your members with bastards . . .
> They taught you the religion they disgraced.
> (1932/1971, pp. 475–476)

People like Langston Hughes, Gwendolyn Brooks, Ralph Ellison, Alice Walker, and others equally articulate could well say that they had shared in this heritage. But it was not determinate for them—at least not in the sense that it prevented them from seeing alternative possibilities of fulfillment for themselves. Not only were they able to mediate their own desires, to identify the reasons for what they chose, even if tradition cried out for telling, even if the past had something to do with the way they felt about themselves and others. Of course, causal forces could be identified in their backgrounds, ways of "explaining" their selection of subject matter, the tones of their voices. But they did not experience outright coercion, for all the doors closed to them. In most cases, they felt and named a gap between what they were and what they desired to be; and, making an intentional effort to cross the gap, knowing it was an alternative to remaining where they were, they felt provisionally free.

A quite different sense of life and range of problems are communicated by the novelist Richard Wright. He was among the artists who tried so hard to give expression to the forms and content of experience forged in the depths of urban life, what Wright called "the Form of Things Unknown." He meant folk sayings, spirituals, blues, work songs, folklore—the hidden substructure of city experience. In one of his essays, Wright talked about the nameless millions who had no voices. And then: "We write out of what life gave us in the form of experience. And there is a value in what we Negro writers say. Is it not clear to you that the American Negro is the only group in our nation that consistently and passionately raises the question of freedom?" And, some years later, Ralph Ellison wrote that the Negro-American represents human values that are unique "in an American way" and can be of value to the whole culture (1952).

Wright's *Native Son* (1940), that remarkable novel about Bigger Thomas, the rejected and frustrated black American who is propelled into murderous violence by conditions he cannot control, presents the issues of freedom in one of the starkest ways we know. It is a presentation, however, that we cannot overlook. Nor, if we are concerned about pluralism, can we set it aside. Many readers can summon up the central scene in the novel, when Mary Dalton (young, radical, friendly to Bigger) gets drunk and asks Bigger to help her to her room. When he is there, her mother comes in; Mary keeps mumbling; Bigger is panicked and tries to silence her so her mother will not find him. He suffocates Mary with a pillow in his panic, "determined she must not move or make any sound that would betray him. His eyes were filled with the white blur moving toward him in the shadows of the room. Again Mary's body heaved and he held the pillow in a grip that took all his strength" (p. 74). He is horrified, incredulous: "Huge words formed slowly, ringing in his ears. She's dead." And later, he decapitates and, in his horror, tries to burn the body.

At his trial, his Marxist lawyer talks about the long history of oppression experienced by Bigger and his people since the days of slavery. The schools had responsibility for the murder, the real estate operators, the "total natural world in which he lives" (p. 333). He murdered without motive; but, afterward, he accepted the crime as "the first full act of his life . . . the most meaningful, exciting and stirring thing that ever happened to him. He accepted it because it made him free, gave him the possibility of choice, of action, the opportunity to act and to feel that his actions carried weight." Then the lawyer continues: "We are dealing here with an impulse stemming from deep down . . . not with how man acts toward man, but with how a man acts when he feels that he must defend himself against, or adapt himself to, the total natural world in which he lives. The central fact to be understood here is not who wronged this boy, but what kind of a vision of the world did he have before his eyes, and where did he get such a vision as to make him, without premeditation, snatch the life of another person so quickly and instinctively that, even though there was an element of accident in it, he was willing after the crime to say: Yes, I did it. I had to." People like

Bigger, the lawyer claims, have the same capacity to live and act as anyone else, but they are not permitted opportunities to express their capacities. Some starve from the lack of self-realization; others murder because of it.

We can return to Sartre's notion of interpretation: Bigger's vision was of a world that had no mercy for him, that would dispose of him as if he were animal if he were found out. It may be that he killed like a brute, unthinkingly, pressured (determined) from without. What he did was caused; and, until he affirmed his own crime, there was nothing to mediate between cause and effect. By distancing, even to the degree of accepting what he had done, thinking about what he had done, he achieved a measure of freedom. Granted, as far as we can know, there was no intention involved in what he did—at least no conscious intention. It is difficult to say, at least in Bigger's case, that the killing of Mary identified certain intentions he had all along. But he did acknowledge the act as his own; and, by doing so, he indicated that, to a degree, he understood himself and that his action had followed bodily and spiritually from the man he was (Ross, 1973, p. 33). So, in some sense, he took responsibility; and, to the degree he did, he could say he was free.

Ralph Ellison's exemplary *Invisible Man* (1952) responds to this at the very start. The narrator is speaking of irresponsibility being part of "invisibility." Then he goes on to ask: "To whom can I be responsible, and why should I be, when you refuse to see me? . . . Responsibility rests upon recognition, and recognition is a form of agreement" (p. 16). He needs to be recognized, as Bigger did. In this case, he needs to be seen not as a member of a race or a class, an ex-college student, an outsider, a Communist recruit, but as an individual. The novel is an account of his search for himself, looking back over 20 years. Also, it is a summary account of black history since emancipation through the beginnings of black nationalism. "It took me a long time," the narrator says, "and much painful boomeranging of my expectations to achieve a realization everyone else appears to have been born with: That I am nobody but myself. But first I had to discover that I am an invisible man!" (p. 19).

The narrator is on a journey, not unfamiliar in the United States. It is evocative of the early settlers', of the pioneers', of Huck Finn's, of Jay Gatsby's. His began (or was, at least, "in the cards") 85 years before, when his grandparents were freed from slavery and were supposed to be united with others "in everything pertaining to the common good, and in everything social, separate like the fingers of the hand." (The remarkable thing about his grandfather, of

course, was that he would play the game of docility while function-
ing "as a spy in enemy country"; and the narrator has known that
since his grandfather died.) His story encompasses black history
from that time, through the "education" in compliance preached by
Booker T. Washington, a forbidden revelation to a white trustee, a
forced journey to New York with false assurances of open opportunity. He works for Liberty Paints as an unintentional strikebreaker,
is "adopted" by the Brotherhood (probably the Communist Party),
has a painful brush with nationalism and rioting in the streets of
Harlem, and at length retreats "underground." Each step of the way,
each instance of "boomeranging" involves him in a tentative out-
reach to some kind of freedom. But then he is expelled from the
Brotherhood for taking initiatives of his own, made (again unintentionally) into an agent of rioting and killing. He is threatened with
hanging by his own people and plunges down a manhole into the
dark.

   His "wall" is the racism of society, along with its manipulations
and labelings. It has also been his incapacity to forge an identity, a
"visibility" for himself, in part because of his alienation from his
origins. Each time he has tried to define a self by means of a project,
he has been subsumed under other people's definitions; his invisibility has been intensified. We are reminded once more that neither the
loss nor the achievement of freedom is attributable to the objective
world around *or* to the person in his/her subjectivity: Merleau-Ponty
has written that there is never absolute determinism and never
absolute choice. "The generality of the 'role' and the situation comes
to the aid of decision, and in this exchange between the situation and
the person who takes it up, it is impossible to determine precisely the
'share contributed by the situation' and the 'share contributed by
freedom'" (1964, p. 453).

   Looked at from a conventional perspective, the situations described in Ellison's novel look as if they are wholly determinate,
leaving the individual no choice at all. How, after all, could he have
resisted the scorn and hatred of a southern white community
aroused by the very words "social responsibility" in a schoolboy's
ritual address? How could he have questioned the values imposed by
a college explicitly interested in letting "the white folks worry about
pride and dignity"? How could he have doubted the promises it
offered (and the devices it taught) when it came to success in the
white man's world? Similar questions might be asked about his
predicament in the paint factory, when he unknowingly helped to
break a strike. Or about his recruitment to the Brotherhood after he

made his indignant speech about eviction and tenants' rights. But the book, as we have seen, is a looking backward, a reinterpreting from a new perspective. It presents what Merleau-Ponty called an "exchange between the situation and the person who takes it up": the narrator's life situation over time and the way he makes sense of it by telling a story about it, imposing form, attaining visibility for himself.

The narrator is underground because all his conceivable options seem to have closed, with the Brotherhood turned against him and the Nationalists dashing through the Harlem streets. Nothing appears viable but finding refuge in a sewer and then in a cellar, nothing but wearing dark glasses as Rinehart does, haunting and subverting and staying out of sight. When, at the end, he decides to stop "hibernating" with the thought that he may, after all, have a "socially responsible role to play," he has endowed the experiences he has suffered with new meanings altogether. He says that "the mind that has conceived a plan of living must never lose sight of the chaos against which that pattern was conceived. That goes for societies as well as individuals" (p. 502). What he speaks of as "chaos" may be the weight of what cannot be changed but can be understood: the deceptions of upward mobility; the plunging "out of history" on the part of so many; the falsifications of ideologies; the dead ends of violence. His determination to invent a "plan of living" represents his refusal to be what the world has made him. And, it may be, because he speaks again of social responsibility, that his plan will bring him into a changed relationship with others to challenge what has been taken for granted and to transform the common world.

The novel, then, may shed a new kind of light on the problem of freedom, especially in our own time. It may be a light from without, a light cast across a "field," since an "invisible man" cannot be absorbed in what is taken to be "normal" or real. He cannot fully "belong," and so his vision remains that of the critical stranger, who always sees more (and differently) than the one habituated to the everyday world. When freedom for most Americans, as Bellah writes, "turns out to mean being left alone by others, not having other people's values, ideas, or styles of life forced upon one, being free of arbitrary authority in work, family, and political life" (1985, p. 23), it becomes especially important to lay bare the old certainties as to what freedom is for. *Invisible Man* enacts a 20-year struggle to be free of others' values, life-styles, authority, and the rest; but it concludes with a painful sense of incompleteness with respect to being "left alone." A socially responsible role, at least for Ellison's character, would involve doing something about building a community of individuals resisting others' manipulations, resisting bonds that (as Bellah writes) "imply obligations that necessarily impinge on one's freedom." Yet, if it is the case that a choice of freedom is a choice of a way of being in the world (Merleau-Ponty, 1962/1967, p. 438), and if being in the world "is somehow correlated with human solidarity," the freedom to be sought is inextricably meshed with responsibility and obligation. No radical reflection, underground or anywhere else, can provide visibility or significance without a deliberate opening to the common.

Ellison's narrator mentions the "chaos" against which a plan of living must be conceived. It is not entirely coincidental that Septima Clark, a schoolteacher who set up Citizenship Schools during the voter registration drives in the south, said that chaos creates "wonderful thinking." She was in no sense underground. She had been dismissed from the Charleston schools because of her membership in the NAACP in the 1950s; and the "wonderful thinking" with which she was concerned had to do with literacy and community for blacks. They were being barred from the polls not only for their inability to read, but by the ludicrous requirements devised by the voting registrars. They required support as well as skills. They needed a sense of being members of a movement that reached far beyond their own localities and polling places. They needed a consciousness of their own dignity and worth in the face of deliberate efforts to incapacitate, frighten, and shame. Like Rosa Parks and others, Septima Clark chose to join a community working slowly and quietly for what we would now call a "pedagogy of the oppressed" in the southern towns. One of Clark's students, Bernice Robinson, taught the first literacy workshop at the Highlander Folk School in 1955, where, as Myles Horton (Highlander's founder) said, "we decided we'd pitch it on a basis of them becoming full citizens and taking their place in society and demanding their rights, and being real men and women in their own right" (Williams, 1987, p. 65).

The world is familiar now with Rosa Parks's refusal to move to the back of the Montgomery bus in 1955, her arrest for breaking the segregation laws, and the bus boycott that followed. It was then that the Reverend Martin Luther King, Jr. freely chose to give up his promising, uneventful career as a pastor and take on the obligation of civil rights. He was elected president of the Montgomery Improvement Association, a post that confirmed him as a primary leader of the burgeoning Civil Rights movement in the south. What is frequently forgotten is that the moments of heroism and transcendence achieved by such people were traceable to the quality of their associations, as well as to their own refusals and demands. Finding freedom repeatedly held away from its objectives (voting, sitting at lunch counters), they came together to name the obstacles—the unjust laws, the segregation codes, the fire hoses, the clubs, the power structures themselves. Having named them, having found them obstacles to their own becoming (no matter how "successful" they were thought to be), they took action together to overcome. They came together, in town after town, on road after road, in "speech and action"; they chose themselves, in all their diversity, as morally responsible for kindred goals. Parks, King, Clark, Abernathy, Evers, Farmer, Lewis, Bond, Jackson, and the thousands of young and old people who marched and suffered for what they had appropriated as cause were pursuing a life project whose name was freedom. They were choosing a way of being in the world.

In one dimension, of course, the struggle was a legal struggle. Fighting for their "rights," the civil rights workers were striving actually for liberty. The segregation laws and the rest were constraints on free action and free speech from without. They took the form of regulations, written and unwritten. They took the form of violence, even when the violence was only implied. When altered by struggle or federal action or courtroom appeals to the Constitution, people were at liberty to sit at lunch counters, drink from water fountains, and attend integrated schools. But the point must be made that, no matter how important the struggle for civil liberties may have been, the freedom with which we are centrally concerned in this discussion is the freedom personally achieved when individuals make decisions they believe to be fully their own. They are decisions, more often than not, based on shared principles or shared conceptions of what is good and right; but they remain decisions personally achieved. It is likely that many of the demonstrations would never have taken place in the south if those addressed in the churches and on the street corners had not chosen freely to participate. At the start, quite obviously, many did not—through indifference, isolation, habitual humility, plain fear. Many were aroused to action by the most eloquent of sermons; numbers (as in the case of the Edmund Pettus Bridge in Selma), by plain indignation, or by the unexpected appearance of supporters from the north. Some, obviously, altered their ways of being in the world by the choices they made during those days.

Much the same can be said about the courageous, frightened children who braved the mobs in New Orleans and Little Rock and other places to integrate the schools. Robert Coles, writing about some of these children in *Children of Crisis* (1967), offered more clues as to how and why living beings reach for their freedom, even in the most fearful circumstances. There was willful Tessie, for instance, who told her Granny that "as bad as they make it for us, the stronger I'll get, because I'll beat them to the punch by imagining it even worse than it is, like I did with that picture I drew the other day" (p. 92). There was John, who found unsuspected strength against the odds, in part because of the "tough side of his personality, the stubborn, crafty, inventive qualities that poor and persecuted people often develop simply to survive." Coles said that those qualities may have "found an event, a challenge that could draw upon them—make them qualities that could guarantee success rather than, as before, keep chaos at arm's length." Then he quoted John: "I'll probably be different the rest of my life" (p. 122).

The Reverend King and other leaders were able to evoke such qualities, it would seem, as they addressed the sense of possibility on the part of those who heard them speak. Certain of their ideas derived from the religious tradition; some, from the conviction that there could indeed be a better social order, that freedom could indeed be attained. There were times when the Reverend King could have argued from a Constitutional point of view. Instead, while arguing for civil disobedience and "redemptive suffering," he appealed to imaginative or intuitive capacities in his audiences. Not only did he inspire them; he relied on their ability to look at things as if they could be otherwise. And he moved them to reach out for a larger personal reality. In his "Letter from a Birmingham Jail," he wrote:

> Oppressed people cannot remain oppressed forever. The yearning for freedom eventually manifests itself, and that is what has happened to the American Negro. Something within has reminded him of his birthright of freedom, and something without has reminded him that it can be gained. Consciously or unconsciously, he has been caught up by the *Zeitgeist*, and with his black brothers of Africa and his brown and yellow brothers of Asia, South America and the Caribbean, the United States Negro is moving with a great urgency toward the promised land of racial justice. (1964, p. 91)

He spoke about the pent-up frustrations and resentments that might be released in other ways if they were not expressed nonviolently. "I have tried to say that this normal and healthy discontent can be channeled into the creative outlet of nonviolent direct action" (p. 93).

The particular moment of nonviolence passed, of course. But we are left with images of multiple communities developing the power to act on perceived possibility. Voting rights were secured; segregation was outlawed in response to a variety of pressures, in addition to the popular movement in the south. It might be said that, although many onlookers were startled and outraged by the extremes of brutality they saw on their television screens, the successes of the Civil Rights movement in the south did not impinge on the welfare or comfort of most whites in the country. In *Eyes on the Prize*, we are told of what occurred when the movement shifted to issues that did not hold the same moral imperative for the nation's moderates—job and housing discrimination, poverty, the Vietnam War. "The movement tackled these varied issues in many varied ways, from black nationalism, black power, and even a call for full-scale revolution to a continuation of marches, protests, court battles, and sit-ins. Nonviolence was no longer the only tool for change; many blacks had seen too many murders, too many betrayals. The built-up anger expressed itself in the 1965 riots in Watts and Harlem, and, later, in Chicago, Detroit, and many other cities. Violence shattered the movement's widespread moral support. The split in the coalition between white liberals and black activists . . . widened dramatically" (Williams, 1987, p. 287). None of the events of later years, even the poverty and joblessness that have afflicted so many, ought to erase the memories of the choices made, the responsibilities undertaken, the project pursued in those years. We discovered much that was possible where the struggle for freedom was concerned; and, later, we discovered more of the complexities, more of the barriers involved.

There have been relatively few novels about the Civil Rights movement, for all the dramatic moments lived through in Albany, Jackson, Birmingham, Montgomery, and the other places in the south. Alice Walker wrote a haunting book called *Meridian* (1976), about a young woman outraged by human suffering, drawn hopelessly to revolution, thinking how important it is to keep singing from memory songs of the people "transformed by the experiences of each generation." At the end, she says her value is to be alone: "Besides, all the people who are as alone as I am will one day gather at the river. We will watch the evening sun go down. And in the darkness maybe we will know the truth" (p. 220). There has been a pulling apart. A full-blown tension has developed between black and white radicals, between those who want to spill blood and those who simply cannot. And, in some sad way, freedom is no longer the point. Some years later, the same Alice Walker wrote *The Color Purple* (1982), in which there is no mention of a popular movement or even a social context. Here the issue is almost purely existential: what it must be like and have been like to have been made into an object by another human being. Celie is victimized in the sense that she can scarcely use the first person singular or the active case when talking about herself. It becomes starkly clear that this kind of experience is linked to an almost total lack of understanding about the lived world; and, without such understanding, freedom appears to be unthinkable.

Celie is, however, enabled to survive and indeed transcend because of the support she receives from the blues singer, Shug Avery, who becomes teacher and sister and friend at once. Through connection, she moves Celie not only to put questions to her familiar world, but to begin to name it and act so that she can transform, through her own actions, her own life. Clearly, she could not have done so alone. One of the moments of release or transcendence is captured when Shug explains to Celie how she freed herself from that "old white man," how she began to feel "part of everything."

> Well, us talk and talk bout God, but I'm still adrift. Trying to chase that old white man out of my head. I been so busy thinking bout him I never truly notice nothing God make. Not a blade of corn (how it do that?) not the color purple (where it come from?) Not the little wildflowers. Nothing.
>
> Now that my eyes are opening, I feels like a fool. Next to any little scrub of a bush in my yard, Mr.——'s evil sort of shrink. But not altogether. Still, it is like Shug say. You have to git man off your eyeball, before you can see anything a'tall. (p. 179)

The words have importance, even pedagogical importance. Celie could not notice the concretely lived world when she was so preoccupied with God, with a remote and pallid authority. Not noticing, she could not question. When she questions, a space opens for her; she knows she has to take initiatives, that she has to name the "man" if she is to see. She has been, in some familiar and deadly way, oppressed. She has internalized the oppressor's vision of herself and, for many years, felt too powerless to move. She may be on the verge when the book ends, but probably only on the verge. There is a family reunion on July 4th, when the family finally gathers. "Why us always have family reunion on July 4th, say Henrietta, mouth poke out, full of complaint. It so hot. White people busy celebrating they independence from England July 4th, say Harpo, so most black folk don't have to work. Us can spend the day celebrating each other" (p. 250). He may be affirming something important about his own people, something that ought to be deeply prized in the American setting; he may be acceding to what, in all its imperfection, simply exists. What, we will have to ask, can freedom signify if it leads to no transformation in the common world? Is it enough, in contemporary America, for persons to be released simply to be?

Our intention is to explore other outsiders' encounters with a world that confronted them very differently than it did the blacks. When we weigh the experiences against one another, we will find the questions multiplying with regard to the nature of freedom in both the private and the public spheres. We will find as well a gathering uncertainty with regard to the relation between pluralism and freedom, pluralism and community, pluralism and a free society. There were illusions once, what Fitzgerald called "the last and greatest of all human dreams"—earlier identified, in relation to Gatsby, as "the service of a vast, vulgar, and meretricious beauty" (1953, p. 99). There was a "melting pot" image; there were images of a great and civil community; there were less enticing images of diverse people "Americanized." Unlike those first comers, the blacks, the newcomers in the nineteenth and twentieth centuries had to be acknowledged as candidates for citizenship, whether or not they fit the preconceived patterns. They had to be initiated into a free society, even though they had to be taught (and many had to be) to be free.

The immigrants, of course, chose to come to this country to escape famine or pogroms or tyrannies or unendurable poverty. As Stephan Thernstrom has pointed out, the late-nineteenth- and early-twentieth-century immigration was selective; and, "as weighed in the scales of the marketplace, those who came—however driven by cruel circumstance—were better adapted to American life than those who remained in the village or died on the way" (1968, p. 61). Moreover, they tended to consider their new situations against standards developed at home. They may have been shocked by their initial experiences, disillusioned to a degree; but their horizons of expectation, as Thernstrom said, were defined by their ethnic and religious cultures, by their Old World traditions, and (at least to some extent) by the degree to which they were "recognized" on these shores.

Most would agree, if asked, that they hoped for freedom of
worship, for a decent living, for some mobility for their children, for
freedom itself. They had come to be free *from* constraints of injustices or natural disasters; and whatever ideas they had for life in a
community or a public were clearly affected by what they knew
before, what they had read, how they had lived. Their experiences of
the ocean crossings were not dissimilar: There was the steerage;
there were the uncertainties of quarantine and Ellis Island; there
were the tests, the threats of separation, the humiliations. For most,
whether they settled in the eastern cities or went in their hopeful
groups toward the west, there were long years of economic tension
and competitiveness. Differences in culture and language, like religious differences, accounted for a slow, uneven growth in the labor
movement, as they did for difficulties in developing class solidarity.
The founders of large corporations, stores, and even universities
discriminated against many of the latecomers even into the twentieth century. That meant, for example, that young intellectuals like
Ludwig Lewisohn and Lionel Trilling suffered obstacles in the way
of their entering into or having careers in English "and made any
thought of a total assimilation into American life not only unrealistic
but lacking in simple dignity" (Howe, 1976, p. 412).

The point, however, for most of the immigrants had to do with
personal and family survival and advancement; and there was a
general assumption that success had to be gained through individual
effort, alone. There were, among the Jews particularly, socialist
groups who wanted to remain together and create a more decent and
equitable society in the new place. Others tried over and over to
break through the barriers of difference by building trade unions.
Certain ones, like Horace Kallen, hoped to see a "cultural pluralism . . . a cooperative of cultural diversities, as a federation or com-
monwealth of national cultures" (1915, pp. 191–192). John Dewey
was preoccupied with "associated or joint activity" among the many,
diverse though they might be, and with the conversion of associated
behavior into communities of action "saturated and regulated by
mutual interest in shared meanings" (1954, p. 151). He wanted the
young to be inducted into the community's traditions and outlook
"by learning in connection with the phenomena of overt association."

Alfred Kazin, in his autobiographical *New York Jew* (1979), tells of
his grandfather wandering about the Lower East Side with a por-
table sewing machine on his shoulder, trying to support a wife and
son. He comments on a letter in the socialist *Jewish Daily Forward*, a

cheerful letter saying, "My heart bounded with joy when I saw New York in the distance. It was like coming to the world city where everything breathed in freedom and where I can become a proletarian." And then, Kazin goes on, "the real word to the worldly wise in America is DO NOT TAKE A MOMENT'S REST; RUN, DO, WORK, AND KEEP YOUR OWN GOOD IN MIND. And this must be my grandfather's word to him—though he is a Socialist" (p. 12). Certainly, in the first generation, this was the dominant view, even among those who needed membership in their own religious or ethnic groups to feel defended against prejudice. There were always those who sought their freedom in rebellion against family ties and controls, in opening their own frontiers on the city streets or out west. Still others found their release in writing. Even amateurs honed their own self-consciousness by writing poetry. Howe writes of the "sweatshop poets" earlier in the century (p. 421 ff.) and calls special attention to Morris Rosenfeld, whose protest carries within it another call to freedom:

> I work, and I work, without rhyme, without reason—
> produce and produce, and produce without end.
> For what? and for whom? I don't know, I don't wonder
> —since when can a whirling machine comprehend?
> Away rush the seconds, the minutes and hours;
> each day and each night like a wind-driven sail;
> I drive the machine, as though eager to catch them,
> I drive without reason—no hope, no avail. . . .
> the clock wakes our senses, and sets us aglow,
> and wakes something else—I've forgotten—don't ask me!
> I'm just a machine, I don't know, I don't know.
>
> (1976, p. 422)

Of course, in context, the poem could be a protest poem, an appeal for improved conditions, even a call for unionization. At once, there is an awareness of gap; there is an insistent questioning: "For what? and for whom?" And there is the potent contradiction that makes the poem open out to freedom: a "whirling machine" cannot comprehend; the fact that the speaker asks, protests, and does not know resists whatever determinism he has in mind.

And, indeed, for growing numbers the conditions of the work required not only seemed to eat away at their freedom, it made them reexamine what seemed to be given and sometimes to reach beyond. Vaguely, perhaps, they felt a hunger not only for having but for being, and for being with others in the world. Harvey Swados, in a story about an Irish schoolteacher come to America to escape the dullness and stagnation at home, writes: "For Kevin, his employment by the automobile factory was like a child's ticket of admission to an awesome, half-believed-in fairyland of new sights, sounds, colors, and odors" (1966, p. 193). Then, as he begins living the reality of the assembly line, he realizes that he may be chained to it for years— "chained to the drudgery, the monotony, the grinding labor—all of which lost their novelty and certainly their glamor when you had won your prize—literally until the prize itself had become valueless and demanded that you replace it with another shinier one" (p. 203). In this case, the disillusioned one goes back to his home country. Others, again, joined unions, built ethnic enclaves, became successful enough to leave the assembly line behind and pursue the "shinier" prize. Novel after novel, however, present individuals preoccupied with a very personal freedom and, more often than not, a very local kind of community. When tragedy comes, it too is intensely personal, as in the case of Geremio, dying in Pietro Di Donato's *Christ in Concrete* (1939), when the cement hardens around him after an accident. "I was born hungry," he thinks, "and have always been hungry for freedom—life! I married and ran away to America so as not to kill and be killed in Tripoli for things they call 'God and Country.' I've never known the freedom I wanted in my heart. There was always an arm upraised to hit at me. What have I done to them? . . . they have cheated me with flags, signs and fear . . . I say you can't take my life! I want to live! My life! To tell the cheated to rise and fight! . . . We must follow the desires within us for the world has been taken from us; we, who made the world" (1939, p. 29). The book is about waste and fragmentation, imbued with the love of family, the love of children, faith in God and in the "Tarantella."

Because Geremio is dying, trapped in fearfully emblematic concrete, he speaks about following the desires within him and his fellow workers. It is unlikely that such outcries were heard in the everyday life of the first-generation immigrant. Few would have said, as Frederick Douglass had, that without resistance there would be no progress; without agitation, no freedom. Exploited as many immigrants were, insulted and humiliated by those of northern European stock, distanced by—and distancing—newcomers like themselves who were of different faiths and different backgrounds, they focused on the material struggle. Few were able to conceive of themselves engaged in quest along with countless others who seemed in many ways so alien, with their remote faiths and their odd perspectives on the world. They were unlikely to speak of moving on to what *they* were not as living beings; they wanted most of all to deal with necessity, to have what was needed to be secure. Thernstrom writes that even those who hoped for and became familiar with the idea of collective action were often impotent: Union leaders themselves "found it hard to keep the other troops in line; a clever Italian-speaking or Polish-speaking foreman could easily exploit national differences for his own ends, and if necessary, there were always the most recent immigrants of all (and the Negroes) to serve as scabs to replace the dissenters en masse" (1968, p. 162).

It remains important to hold in mind the ways in which lived experiences differed nonetheless from group to group. The strains of cultural clash and adaptation have always had different meanings, depending on class, pride in family, level of mobility. We might think of the Irish Studs Lonigan, desperate for "respectability" as he seeks work during the Depression: "I'll tell you, stranger, it's a dirty shame when you and I and our type have to take it on the chin. Take myself now. I get pretty damn sore when I think of what I had. A swell apartment out on Wilson Avenue, gals, all the wine, women, and song my little heart desired, and a nice wad socked away. Nothing in the world to disturb my peace of mind, or my night's rest. And then, the firm goes bust, the bank closes its doors, so here I am. But I ain't through not by a damn sight. I was in the class once, and that's where I'll be again" (Farrell, 1934/1944, p. 361). There were the ones who found their projects in ward politics, the ones who became union leaders or tugboat captains or balladeers. Later, there were radicals like William Z. Foster and Elizabeth Gurley Flynn (even as there had been strikebreakers like the Molly McGuires preceding them). Flynn was called by Theodore Dreiser the "East Side Joan of Arc." She wrote that the "awareness of being Irish came to us as small children through plaintive song and heroic story. . . . We drew in a burning hatred of British rule with our mother's milk" (1955, p. 13). Most remained proletarians but found it harder and harder to retain that distinctly Irish identity over the years, in spite of their schools and churches, in spite of the Protestant contempt that afflicted so many. Eventually, there were John F. Kennedy and those around him, the educated and the startlingly wealthy, articulating out of a past of ward politics a politics of possibility. More recently, there were the outraged "townies" on the South Side of Boston, declaring their difference by defying both the "limousine liberals" and the advancing blacks.

Neighborhoods, enclaves, loyalties, separations. There were class distinctions as well, often making it difficult, as the years went on, to move in search of freedom and a "common ground." The spectrum may have been longest of all among the Jewish immigrants in their several waves. There were barriers and quotas; Jews were caricatured; some clung to the distinctiveness of orthodoxies; others yearned for the freedoms cosmopolitanism and assimilation ought to have brought. Rising in the socio-economic scale, moving through the cities to better and better neighborhoods, numerous Jews equated freedom from persecution with business and professional success. At various times, they were the prime movers of radical groups and movements, although always in the minority among their fellow Jews. Often their radicalism was defined in the context of European traditions. Little attention was paid, because their ideas lacked reference to the American community as it had grown and declined and reformed itself over the years. They committed themselves often to a worldwide community, frequently of the working class or the oppressed. Because of their own long traditions of literacy, they invested in education, thrusting open whatever doors they could find. Sometimes education meant generational revolt for them: the narratives, especially of Jewish males, are filled with rebellions against old-country structures, conservative fathers, mothers imposing possessive love. In the 1960s, Jewish youth were prominent in the campus protests, the peace movement, Mississippi Summer. Most were middle-class, demonstrating the hollowness of consumerism and ambition, seeking identifications with groups and communities not entirely their own. The European Holocaust and the founding of Israel presumably provided a new group identity; but, as each generation appeared, there were more and more subdivisions among the Jews. Certain ones were due to social class; others, to religious belief; still others, to the degree of Zionism and militancy.

Even today, in the loosely woven textures of some of their communities, Jews remain individualists, sometimes treading cautiously, still uncertain of their identity. There is Saul Bellow's "dangling man," strange in the world; there is his Augie March "going everywhere," wanting to be adopted, wanting to be a "Columbus of the near-at-hand" (1939). There are the new incarnations of Jewish folk culture in Bernard Malamud's works—the good and suffering people in their tenement rooms, their grocery stores, on city streets. In *The Assistant* (1957), the hard-driven grocer, Morris Bober, is too desperately involved in his own struggle for existence to say to anyone else, especially an enemy, that he suffers for him. In Philip Roth's novels, people resentfully or outrageously deny and affirm their Jewishness in a world that increasingly does not care. In Norman Mailer's work, the very self-dramatizations with respect to "others" (be those others black people, New England poets, Puerto Rican fighters, peace demonstrators in the "armies of the night") are reminders of alienation and separateness, a perhaps fated search for what freedom is *for*.

The experiences of the various groups differed deeply, even within the same lived world. The Irish, developing talents in political bureaucracies before the others, have had different approaches to work, different hopes for upward mobility. Restive in the face of Protestant and Jewish liberalism, many were supporters of McCarthyism, as many (although not all) today are opponents of gay rights, abortion, and the rest. Daniel Moynihan has written that the artists and intellectuals born in Irish-Catholic environments have rejected their origins as hostile to their aspirations; but he still envisions an emergence of an intellectual class "encouraged by the Church and sustained by the increasing relevance of religious doctrine to the intellectual concerns of the present age" (Glazer & Moynihan, 1964/ 1973, p. 278). Much depends on the education Catholics receive; and questions are continually raised with regard to the quality and cost of Catholic schools. Much depends as well on the ways in which Catholics interpret their situations in the increasingly problematic world they inhabit along with others, the degree to which theologies of liberation become incarnated as yearnings for new kinds of freedom in a pluralist domain, the degree to which Catholics can come together with others and take part in an authentically public space.

When we ponder the full range of perspectives on the part of newcomers arriving here at various times in history, when we ponder their differential approaches to education and to possibility generally, we are likely to find a kind of irony in the schools' emphasis on assimilation and Americanization over the years. For many, it is true, the early grades of school have been taken by many entering groups to be doorways to a mainstream that many newly arrived adults did not understand. Basic skills were taught under rigorous circumstances in the first decades of the century. The average immigrant child had no contact with progressive teachers eager to help him/her release particular preferences and develop into a thinking person in the midst of a friendly community. Even if the child had such contact, it is doubtful whether his/her ethnic or religious distinctiveness would have been noted or valued; since the dominant concern was to usher all children into the ways of life and thinking associated with the society as it existed. For many years, the difficulties of foreign-language speakers were thought of as deficiencies on the part of children in some way inferior. The numbers of Hispanic children in the cities, coupled with political pressures and a slow growth of attentiveness to "multiculturalism," finally led to some interest in bilingualism. Support for it seems to be diminishing again, as attention shifts to "common learnings," "higher-order skills," and the technical literacies presumably required for an advanced technological society.

We cannot but think back to such educators as the New York City superintendent Julia Richman, herself a German Jew, who made brashly clear where she thought the public schools should stand when it came to fitting children into the system. Their parents, she once said, "must be made to understand what it is we are trying to do for the children. They must be made to realize that in forsaking the land of their birth, they were also forsaking the customs and traditions of that land; and they must be made to realize an obligation, in adopting a new country, to adopt the language and customs of that country" (Tyack, 1974, p. 237). She sounded very like the teacher in Harriette Arnow's *The Dollmaker*, who so bitterly scorns Gertie Nevels for saying how it was "back home." The teacher hisses at her: "You hill-southerners who come here, don't you realize before you come that it will be a great change for your children? For the better of course, but still a change" (p. 322).

That, in many respects, was the point. The Americanizing process, the process of induction itself, the lines in the school corridors, the tracking and grouping systems, the factory atmospheres, the racist, sexist, classist practices: All were justified on some level by a promise of membership with the benefits that was supposed to entail. To be a citizen of a "free society"—self-controlled, God-fearing, patriotic, hard-working, law-abiding—was to have solved the problem of freedom. Today, confronting what many view as the excesses of freedom (what with the AIDS epidemic, the adolescent pregnancies, the young people's street crimes, the addictions), administrators and officials call for abstinence, discipline, increased control.

There are, there have always been, refusals and resistances. There have been tensions involving group after group. Italian parents, for instance, especially those from the south of Italy, had no great faith in schooling. As we know from Leonard Covello's autobiography (1958), they required their children to go to work early and contribute to the family's upkeep. They were determined to keep them within the family circle and in whatever constituted the family business, to prevent them from assimilating fully, to keep their subculture alive. Covello wrote of the embarrassment he was made to feel in school and of his efforts to keep his mother, with her shawl and her Italian accent, away; and, clearly, he was not alone. John Fante's "The Odyssey of a Wop" is full of pain and shame, even at his father's pictures of the cathedral of Milan and St. Peter's. His father boasts of his heirlooms—the beautiful wine-pitcher, the Italian king's photograph. "So I begin to shout at him. I tell him to cut out being a Wop and be an American once in a while" (Fante, 1966, pp. 393–394). Fante at length identifies with his father and, at least spiritually, goes home again. Covello, with the encouragement of friends, went back to the school he had left, went on to Columbia, and became an educator himself. His first post was teaching Italian; his first commitment, to instill pride in Italian culture and the Italian language in those who, like himself, had been shamed. It may be said that Covello's eventual career—instituting bilingual education, establishing storefront centers and community councils, trying to mediate gang fights among those he called the "powerless," struggling to direct the energy used up in violence to collective action—was the career of someone who broke free.

He was probably exceptional; because so many immigrants and children of immigrants remained in their enclaves, struggling above all to survive. Most did not question the system, even in its inequity and brutality; if they were skilled enough, cunning enough, hard-working enough, they would get what they needed within the system. They did not experience it as concrete; even when its representatives demeaned them and discriminated against them, they assumed it was up to them and to those nearest them to surmount or evade the wall. Almost never did they name theirs to be a "common lot" they shared with other newcomers. Even the early unions could not move them to cross the gulfs between the groups. If they were members of the working class, or small businesspeople, or street vendors, they took pride in "making it" by themselves and for themselves. They did not experience the system itself, or its structures or its agencies, as giving rise to barriers that could not be negotiated somehow. And, more often than not, they felt totally alienated from the very poor, the "underclass," the ones on welfare, the ones who depended on others for support.

There is no question but that this country has been able to absorb newcomers with comparative ease; and most of them, in time, have done more than simply survive. They would say, if asked, that the schooling provided for their children was the kind of schooling necessary in this country, except where industrial dislocations or discriminatory practices have rendered the alluring promises false. When we look abroad and see the ethnic conflicts flaring, the religious massacres, the race riots, apartheid, we cannot but affirm the strength of our system and the degree of civil peace, for all the fragmentation, for all the erosions of community. We can affirm the degree of pluralism we have achieved as well, even as we point (as we must) to the deficiencies. And, indeed, there are multiple deficiencies, some of them remediable: the increasing distances between groups; the persisting racisms; the competing claims; the acquiescence to the rationalizations, the cheerful formulas, the quantifications, the simplifications. There is even something reminiscent of what Hannah Arendt (borrowing from Bertolt Brecht) once called "dark times" (1968, p. viii). They were marked, she said, by "highly efficient talk and double-talk" of officials who "explained away unpleasant facts and justified concerns," by a camouflage spread by the establishment or the system. If it is the function of the public realm to throw light on human affairs by providing a space where persons can show "in deed and word, for better and worse, who they are and what they can do," dark times have come when that light is put out by credibility gaps and invisible government, "by speech that does not disclose what is but sweeps it under the carpet, by exhortations, moral and otherwise, that, under the pretext of upholding old truths, degrade all truth to meaningless triviality." And, more often than not, it is not visible to people who ought to have learned to see.

Whether it is mystification by the media, a cynicism due to the wars and corruptions of the recent past, a wishful thinking, an unquenchable desire for comfort and for certainty, Americans generally do not perceive the "darkness" Arendt described; nor do they perceive the significance of a public space that might throw light. Nor, in addition, do they see the connection between efforts to create such a space among themselves and the pursuit of freedom. It is all too clear that very few people today conceive of themselves as engaged in a quest along with others who have different faiths and different perspectives on the world. It is certainly true, as we have said, that individuals and families preoccupied with basic survival needs can scarcely attend to calls to freedom of this kind. But there are thousands upon thousands whose basic needs have long since been met and who nonetheless focus on material satisfactions and possessions, no matter how artificial the needs now being fulfilled, no matter how much "superfluity" characterizes their lives. In an odd way, even the more well-to-do are evocative of young Antoine Bloyé, described earlier, the boy who believed that people with incomes are the only ones who enjoy "a form of freedom." It is not only the limitation and sterility of a negative view of freedom; it is the decision to let the system carry them, to let themselves be impelled and compelled. As in the case of Antoine Bloyé, for a person like this, there is almost no opportunity to "think about himself, to meditate, to know himself and know the world." Worse, "the springs of his life, and the drive of his actions were not within himself" (Nizan, 1973, p. 113).

The seriousness of this is not "only personal," if the idea of "hard times" is taken to be relevant at all. It has to do with the very climate and substance of our society today; it may even have to do with the survival of our democracy. And it may be that we no longer know how to create the kinds of situations in which persons are likely to choose themselves as committed and as free. As we have said, they may have the liberty to speak, to buy books, to change jobs, to leave home; but they do not know what it is to reach out for freedom as a palpable good, to engage with and resist the compelling and conditioning forces, to open fields where the options can multiply, where unanticipated possibilities open each day. Nor do they see the relation between their pursuit and the opening of a public space where persons can appear before one another as who they are and what they can do. We have seen how different the situation is when people are experiencing slavery or segregation or totalitarian rule. For many of them, it begins to seem impossible to breathe without achieving freedom; so they come together deliberately to make the necessary space. When they do so, they are acting and experiencing quite differently than they would if, as separate individuals, they took off for an escape up the river, across the border, toward the frontier.

Merleau-Ponty has written about how long it often takes for people to perceive their lives as synchronized with others in the same predicament, to realize that "all share a common lot" (1962/ 1967, p. 444). Also, he wrote that it takes an easing of living conditions for the horizon to open, to be no longer restricted to immediate concerns. There must be, he said, "economic play and room for a new project in relation to living." The project, an existential one, can take shape only "on a certain basis of co-existence." With only a few exceptions in our history, Americans (old settlers and newcomers) have not known that basis of co-existence, any more than they have known what solidarity signifies. In most cases, since freedom has to do with private existence, associated efforts were viewed as means of attaining private ends. They have been viewed as means of resisting power, usually understood as a manipulation, a form of hegemony, an imposition of a ruler's word.

For Michel Foucault, power is actually a question of government; it refers to the ways in which individual or group conduct may be directed—in schools, in communities, in hospitals. He wrote that government originally meant the creation of "an open field of possibilities" or a political space for possible action, a public space of possibilities (1984, p. 221). Freedom, for Foucault, is a basic requisite for action and for power, since "power is exercised only over free subjects and only insofar as they are free." When we think of the diverse and pluralist society we have been describing, we need then to have in mind a range of individuals or groups confronting a field of possibilities in which varied ways of behaving and reacting may be realized. Against such a background, power and action cannot but resist doctrines of determinism and fatalism, or (as Foucault writes) what reverberates in "social-scientific behaviorism." For Hannah Arendt as well, there are crucial connections between power, freedom, and the public space: Freedom, for her as for the ancient Greek philosophers, is located in the public realm. For her, the backbone of this realm is what she called human "plurality," recognized as "the basic condition of both action and speech" (1958, pp. 155–156; 179–180). In describing that plurality, she said it has the twofold character of "equality and distinction." Without equality, there could be no public space; and she meant by that, of course, equality of regard. Without distinctiveness or uniqueness, people would have no need for speech or action to make themselves understood; because, if they were all identical, mere signs or gestures would be enough.

The matter of freedom, then, in a diverse society is also a matter of power, as it involves the issue of a public space. There have been voices, as we have seen, articulating the connections between the individual search for freedom and appearing before others in an open place, a public and political sphere. There have been those who saw the relation between participation and individual development, between finding one's voice and creating a self in the midst of other selves. There have been those who have named the obstacle to their own becoming in self-regard, in indifference, in lack of mutuality and care. How, in a society like ours, a society of contesting interests and submerged voices, an individualist society, a society still lacking an "in-between," can we educate for freedom? And, in educating for freedom, how can we create and maintain a common world?

CHAPTER 5

Education, Art, and Mastery: Toward the Spheres of Freedom

Our exploration began in an awareness of a taken-for-grantedness and a void where present-day thinking is concerned, of a lassitude and a lack of care. The void exists with regard to the question of freedom, the givenness of which is taken for granted. We have, in the course of this inquiry, distinguished freedom from liberty for the purpose of highlighting the tension and the drama of personal choosing in an intersubjective field—choosing among others in a conditioned world. Liberty may be conceived of in social or political terms: Embodied in laws or contracts or formulations of human rights, it carves out a domain where free choices can be made. For Isaiah Berlin, the sense of freedom entails "the absence of obstacles to possible choices and activities—absence of obstructions on roads along which a man can decide to walk" (1970, p. xxxix). We recognize, as he did, that among the obstructions to be removed (and preferably through social action) are those raised by poverty, sickness, even ignorance. We recognize as well that the removal of obstacles to "possible choices and activities" may, in many cases, lead to domination by the few and the closing off of opportunities for the many. We know too that, even given conditions of liberty, many people do not act on their freedom; they do not risk becoming different; they accede; often, they submit.

The problems for education, therefore, are manifold. Certain ones cluster around the presumed connection between freedom and

autonomy; certain ones have to do with the relation between freedom and community, most significantly moral community. Autonomy, many believe, is a prime characteristic of the educated person.
To be autonomous is to be self-directed and responsible; it is to be
capable of acting in accord with internalized norms and principles; it
is to be insightful enough to know and understand one's impulses,
one's motives, and the influences of one's past. There are those who
ascribe to the autonomous person a free rational will, capable of
making rational sense of an extended objective world. Values like
independence, self-sufficiency, and authenticity are associated with
autonomy, because the truly autonomous person is not supposed to
be susceptible to outside manipulations and compulsions. Indeed, he/
she can, by maintaining a calm and rational stance, transcend compulsions and complexes that might otherwise interfere with judgment and clarity.

As is well known, the attainment of autonomy characterizes the
highest state in the developmental patterns devised by Jean Piaget
(1977) and, later, by Lawrence Kohlberg (1971). Piaget saw autonomy as emergent from experience of mutual reciprocity and regard.
A life plan, he wrote, is "an affirmation of autonomy"; and "a life
plan is above all a scale of values which puts some ideals above others
and subordinates the middle-range values to goals thought of as
permanent" (p. 443). For Kohlberg, whose primary interest was in
moral development, people who reach a high-enough cognitive stage
of development become autonomous enough to guide their choices
by universalizable principles of justice and benevolence. "That welfare and justice," he said, "are guiding principles of legislation as well
as of individual moral action points to the fact that a principle is
always a maxim or a rule for making rules or laws as well as a maxim
of individual situational conduct" (p. 60). If the presumption is that
autonomy is associated with "higher order" thinking and with the
ability to conceptualize abstractions like human rights and justice,
and if indeed such principles become maxims of individual conduct,
many conclude that autonomous persons can be considered free
persons. To abide by internalized principles, after all, is to acknowledge the rule of "ought" or "should." R. M. Hare has written that it
is because we *can* act in this way or that, that we ask whether we
ought to do this or that (1965, p. 51ff.). Granting the various usages
of words like "ought" and "should," we can still understand why
persons who are capable of principled action and who are responsive
to ideals they have incarnated for themselves are considered self-
determining and therefore free.

The implications for education have had to do with cognition—with logical thinking, the resolution of moral dilemmas, the mastery of interpersonal rules. For R. S. Peters, this kind of education involves the nurture of a "rational passion" associated with commitment to the worthwile. Peters wrote: "Respect for truth is intimately connected with fairness, and respect for persons, which together with freedom, are fundamental principles which underlie our moral life and which are personalized in the form of the rational passions" (1970, p. 55). The problem with this highly cognitive focus in the classroom has in part to do with what it excludes. Also, it has to do with whether or not reasoning is enough when it comes to acting in a resistant world, or opening fields of possibilities among which people may choose to choose. There have been many reports on classroom discussions of issues ostensibly of moment to the students: cheating, betraying confidences, nonviolent resistance, sexual relations, discrimination. Not only has there been little evidence that the participants take such issues personally; there has been little sign of any transfer to situations in the "real world," even when there were opportunities (say, in a peace demonstration) to act on what were affirmed as guiding principles. We will touch, before long, on the importance of imagination and the exploration of alternative possibilities. It seems clear, as Oliver and Bane have said, that young people "need the opportunity to project themselves in rich hypothetical worlds created by their own imagination or those of dramatic artists. More important, they need the opportunity to test out new forms of social order—and only then to reason about their moral implications" (1971, p. 270).

Most of the writers to whom we have referred in these paragraphs are, of course, interested primarily in moral commitments, not freedom *per se*. It does appear, as has been said, that there is a presupposition linking autonomy to personal freedom, autonomy in the sense of rational and principled self-government. For many, a movement out of heteronomous existence, with all its conditioning and shaping factors, cannot but be a movement in the direction of a kind of rule-governed self-sufficiency and independence. And this (at least where qualified students are concerned) is viewed by numbers of educators as the most desirable end of pedagogy, to be achieved by liberal education and commitment to the worthwhile.

Such inquiries into women's moral development as Carol Gilligan's *In a Different Voice* (1981) and into women's distinctive modes of reflection as *Women's Ways of Knowing* by Mary Field Belenky and her colleagues (1986) have, at the very least, made problematic the focal emphasis on separateness and responsiveness to purely formal principle. Gilligan has pointed time and time again to the neglect of the patterns of women's development, whose "elusive mystery . . . lies in its recognition of the continuing importance of attachment in the human life cycle. Woman's place in man's life cycle is to protect this recognition while the developmental litany intones the celebration of separation, autonomy, individuation, and natural rights" (p. 23). Belenky's work emphasizes the relational thinking and the integration of voices that characterize women's life stories. Where freedom is concerned (and it is rarely mentioned in contemporary women's literature), it is taken to signify either liberation from domination or the provision of spaces where choices can be made. There is a general acknowledgment that the opening of such spaces depends on support and connectedness. "Connected teaching," for example, involves what Nel Noddings describes as "care" (1984, pp. 15–16). Rather than posing dilemmas to students or presenting models of expertise, the caring teacher tries to look through students' eyes, to struggle *with* them as subjects in search of their own projects, their own ways of making sense of the world. Reflectiveness, even logical thinking remain important; but the *point* of cognitive development is not to gain an increasingly complete grasp of abstract principles. It is to interpret from as many vantage points as possible lived experience, the ways there are of being in the world.

This recent attentiveness to mutuality and to responsiveness to others' wants and concerns cannot but recall the contextual thinking of Dewey, Merleau-Ponty, Hannah Arendt, Michel Foucault, and others. Dewey wrote of the habit of viewing sociality as a trait of an individual "isolated by nature, quite as much as, say, a tendency to combine with others in order to get protection against something threatening one's own private self" (1938/1963, p. 22). He believed it essential to consider the problem of freedom within the context of culture, surely within a context of multiple transactions and relationships. Part of the difficulty for him and those who followed him had to do with the positing of a "free will" associated with a mysterious interiority, even as it had to do with a decontextualization that denied the influences of associated life. Hannah Arendt found some of the century's worst contradictions in the distinction made between "inner" freedom and the kind of outward "unfreedom" or causality described by Immanuel Kant and his successors. The search for a freedom within, she said, denied notions of *praxis* and the public space. For her, as we have seen, freedom was identified with a space that provided room for human action and interaction. She believed that freedom was the major reason persons came together in political orders; it is, she wrote, "the *raison d'être* of politics" and the opposite of "inner freedom," which she called "the inward space into which we may escape from external coercion and *feel* free" (1961, pp. 141–146).

The relationships and responsibilities stressed by women inquirers are not to be identified entirely with the cultural matrix of such importance to Dewey; nor is either emphasis precisely the same as Arendt's concern with the public space. Nonetheless, all these strains of thought are significant responses to present calls, in philosophy and the human sciences, for some reconstitution of core values, some rebuilding of community today. Attention is being repeatedly called to the crucial good of "friendship" in the Aristotelian qualitative-moral sense (see *Nichomachean Ethics*, Bk. VIII)—the relation between those who desire the good of friends for their friends' sake, no matter how different that "good" may be from what a companion chooses and pursues. In some degree, this is a way of acknowledging and respecting another's freedom to choose among possibilities, as it involves a desire to foster that choosing, because the other is a friend. There is talk of "solidarity" as well, as in the case of Richard Rorty talking about human beings giving sense to their lives by placing them in a larger context. There are two ways of doing this, he says: "by telling the story of their contribution to a community" or "by describing themselves as standing in immediate relation to a nonhuman reality." He calls the first story an example of the desire for solidarity, the second an example of the desire for objectivity. "Insofar as a person is seeking solidarity, he or she does not ask about the relation between the practices of the chosen community and something outside that community" (1985, p. 3). Rorty associates the notion of solidarity with pragmatism, especially when the suggestion is made that the only foundation for the sense of community is "shared hope and the trust created by such sharing." This removes not only objectivism but absoluteness; it returns us to the ideas of relatedness, communication, and disclosure, which provide the context in which (according to the viewpoint of this book) freedom must be pursued.

It is because of people's embeddedness in memory and history, because of their incipient sense of community, that freedom in education cannot be conceived either as an autonomous achievement or as merely one of the principles underlying our moral life, personalized (as R. S. Peters said) "in the form of rational passions." It is because of the apparent normality, the givenness of young people's everyday lives, that intentional actions ought to be undertaken to bring things within the scope of students' attention, to make situations more palpable and visible. Only when they are visible and "at hand" are they likely to cry out for interpretation. And only when individuals are empowered to interpret the situations they live together do they become able to mediate between the object-world and their own consciousness, to locate themselves so that freedom can appear.

Aware of how living persons are enmeshed, engaged with what surrounds them, Merleau-Ponty wrote:

> It is because we are through and through compounded of relationships with the world that for us the only way to become aware of the fact is to suspend the resultant activity . . . to put it out of play. Not because we reject the certainties of common sense and a natural attitude to things—they are, on the contrary, the consistent theme of philosophy—but because, being the presupposed basis of any thought, they are taken for granted and go unnoticed, and because in order to arouse them and bring them into view we have to suspend for a moment our recognition of them. (1962/1967, p. xiii)

He was not talking about withdrawing into some interior domain. Nor was he calling for a deflection of attention from ordinary life. Rather, he was exploring the possibilities of seeing what was ordinarily obscured by the familiar, so much part of the accustomed and the everyday that it escaped notice entirely. We might think about the clocks that play such important parts in schoolrooms, or school bells, or loudspeakers blaring at the beginning and end of the day; about calling individual children "third graders" or "lower track"; about threats to summon the remote principal; even about the Pledge of Allegiance, and about the flags drooping in the public rooms. Why *should* these phenomena be presupposed as a "basis" for thought and self-identification? We might think of the way the chalkboard is placed, of the peculiar distancing of the teacher at the front desk, of books firmly shut before the reading is done. The point is to find a means of making all this an object of thought, of critical attention. And we may be reminded again of Foucault's remark that "thought is freedom in relation to what one does." Part of the effort might be to defamiliarize things, to make them strange. How would a Martian view what was there, a "boat person" newly arrived? What would happen if the hands were removed from the clock? (No one, for instance, who has read William Faulkner's *The*

Sound and the Fury is likely to forget the strangeness of what happens when Quentin pulls the hands off his watch on the day of his suicide. "Hearing it, that is," thinks Quentin, "I don't suppose anybody ever deliberately listens to a watch or a clock. You don't have to. You can be oblivious to the sound for a long while, then in a second of ticking it can create in the mind unbroken the long diminishing parade of time you didn't hear" [1946, p. 96]. Later, he remembers that "Father said clocks slay time. He said time is dead as long as it is being clicked off by little wheels; only when the clock stops does time come to life" [p. 104]. Reading that, one cannot but find the clock-field, the clock-world, expanding. And the possibilities of thinking multiply.) What of paper? Why is there so much paper? So many files? (George Konrad's novel about a Hungarian social worker, called *The Case-worker*, also makes a reader see—and ask, and question. "I question, explain, prove, disprove, comfort, threaten, grant, deny, demand, approve. . . . The order I defend is brutal though fragile, it is un-pleasant and austere; its ideas are impoverished and its style is lacking in grace. . . . I repudiate the high priests of individual salva-tion and the sob sisters of altruism, who exchange commonplace partial responsibility for the aesthetic transports of cosmohistorical guilt or the gratuitous slogans of universal love. I refuse to emulate these Sunday-school clowns and prefer—I know my limitations—to be the sceptical bureaucrat that I am. My highest aspiration is that a medium-rank, utterly insignificant civil servant should, as far as possible, live with his eyes open" [1974, p. 168]. Again, familiar bureaucratic orders in one's own world thrust themselves into vis-ibility. Seeing more, feeling more, one reaches out for more to do.)

Walker Percy's narrator in *The Moviegoer* says it in another way. He is trying to relieve his own boredom, a boredom verging on despair; and the idea of a search suddenly occurs to him.

> What is the nature of the search? you ask.
>
> Really, it is very simple, at least for a fellow like me; so simple that it is easily overlooked.
>
> The search is what anyone would undertake if he were not sunk in the everydayness of his own life. This morning, for example, I felt as if I had come to myself on a strange island. And what does such a castaway do? Why, he pokes around the neighborhood and he doesn't miss a trick.
>
> To become aware of the possibility of the search is to be onto something. Not to be onto something is to be in despair. (1979, p. 13)

To undertake a search is, of course, to take an initiative, to refuse stasis and the flatness of ordinary life. Since the narrator says he was "sunk in everydayness," his search is clearly for another perspective, one that will disclose what he has never seen. Even to realize that he can be "onto something" is to begin perceiving lacks in his own life. The question as to what the "neighborhood" holds and implies remains open. He may be moved to "poke around" because others have taken heed of him, because he has appeared in the open for almost the first time. If this is so, he may acquire the space that will free him from his environment of everydayness. The experience may be one denoting a willingness "to learn again to see the world"—and to restore "a power to signify, a birth of meaning, or a wild meaning, an expression of experience by experience" (Merleau-Ponty, 1962/1967, p. 60). I am suggesting that there may be an integral relationship between reaching out to learn to learn and the "search" that involves a pursuit of freedom. Without being "onto something," young people feel little pressure, little challenge. There are no mountains they particularly want to climb, so there are few obstacles with which they feel they need to engage. They may take no heed of neighborhood shapes and events once they have become used to them—even the figures of homelessness, the wanderers who are mentally ill, the garbage-strewn lots, the burned-out buildings. It may be that no one communicates the importance of thinking about them or suggests the need to play with hypothetical alternatives. There may be no sense of identification with people sitting on the benches, with children hanging around the street corners after dark. There may be no ability to take it seriously, to take it personally. Visible or invisible, the world may not be problematized; no one aches to break through a horizon, aches in the presence of the question itself. So there are no tensions, no desires to reach beyond.

There is an analogy here for the passivity and the disinterest that prevent discoveries in classrooms, that discourage inquiries, that make even reading seem irrelevant. It is not simply a matter of motivation or interest. In this context, we can call it a question having to do with freedom or, perhaps, the absence of freedom in our schools. By that I do not necessarily mean the ordinary limits and constraints, or even the rules established to ensure order. I mean, in part, the apparent absence of concern for the ways in which young people feel conditioned, determined, even *fated* by prevailing circumstances. Members of minority groups, we are repeatedly informed, do not see the uses of commitment to schooling and studying. No matter how they yearn for success in society, they are convinced of inimical forces all around them, barricades that cannot be overcome. Poor children and others often experience the weight of what is

called "cultural reproduction," although they cannot name it or resist
it. By that is meant not only the reproduction of ways of knowing,
believing, and valuing, but the maintenance of social patternings and
stratifications as well. The young people may not chafe under the
inequities being kept alive through schools, as inequities often are;
they are likely to treat them as wholly "normal," as predictable as
natural laws. The same might be said about advantaged children who
grow up with a sense of entitlement and privilege, but still feel they
have no choice.

The challenge is to engage as many young people as possible in
the thought that is freedom—the mode of thought that moved Sarah
Grimké, Elizabeth Cady Stanton, Septima Clark, Leonard Covello,
the Reverend King, and so many others into action. Submergence
and the inability to name what lies around interfere with questioning and learning. Dewey had something much like this in mind when
he emphasized the dangers of "recurrence, complete uniformity,"
"the routine and mechanical" (1934, p. 272). What he sometimes
called the "anaesthetic" in experience is what numbs people and
prevents them from reaching out, from launching inquiries. For
Dewey, experience becomes fully conscious only when meanings
derived from earlier experience enter in through the exercise of the
imaginative capacity, since imagination "is the only gateway through
which these meanings can find their way into a present interaction;
or rather . . . the conscious adjustment of the new and the old *is*
imagination" (p. 272). The word, the concept "conscious" must be
emphasized. Experience, for Dewey, becomes "human and conscious" only when what is "given here and now is extended by
meanings and values drawn from what is absent in fact and present
only imaginatively." Conscious thinking always involves a risk, a
"venture into the unknown"; and it occurs against a background of
funded or sedimented meanings that must themselves be tapped and
articulated, so that the mind can continue dealing consciously and
solicitously with lived situations, those situations (as Dewey put it)
"in which we find ourselves" (p. 263).

Education for freedom must clearly focus on the range of
human intelligences, the multiple languages and symbol systems
available for ordering experience and making sense of the lived
world. Dewey was bitterly opposed to the anti-intellectual tendencies in the culture and frequently gave voice to what he called "a plea
for casting off that intellectual timidity which hampers the wings of
imagination, a plea for speculative audacity, for more faith in ideas,
sloughing off a cowardly reliance upon those partial ideas to which

we are wont to give the name facts" (1931, p. 12). He spoke often as well about the kinds of inquiry that deliberately challenge desires for certainty, for fixity. He would undoubtedly have agreed with John Passmore's more recent call for "critico-creative thinking," the kind that is consciously norm-governed but at once willing to challenge rules that become irrelevant or stultifying. No principle, Passmore wrote, no person or text or work of art should be kept beyond the reach of rational criticism. There should nonetheless be a continuing initiation into the great traditions in which we are all, whether we are aware of it or not, embedded. Passmore went on:

> Critical thinking as it is exhibited in the great traditions conjoins imagi-
> nation and criticism in a single form of thinking; in literature, science,
> history, philosophy or technology, the free flow of the imagination is
> controlled by criticism and criticisms are transformed into a new way of
> looking at things. Not that either the free exercise of the imagination or
> the raising of objections is in itself to be despised; the first can be
> suggestive of new ideas, the second can show the need for them. But
> certainly education tries to develop the two in combination. The educa-
> tor is interested in encouraging critical discussion as distinct from the
> mere raising of objections; and discussion is an exercise of the imagina-
> tion. (1975, p. 33)

A concern for the critical and the imaginative, for the opening of new ways of "looking at things," is wholly at odds with the technicist and behaviorist emphases we still find in American schools. It represents a challenge, not yet met, to the hollow formulations, the mystifications so characteristic of our time. We have taken note of the forms of evangelism and fundamentalism, the confused uneasiness with modernism that so often finds expression in anti-intellectualism or an arid focus on "Great Books." Given the dangers of small-mindedness and privatism, however, I do not think it sufficient to develop even the most variegated, most critical, most imaginative, most "liberal" approach to the education of the young. If we are seriously interested in education for freedom as well as for the opening of cognitive perspectives, it is also important to find a way of developing a *praxis* of educational consequence that opens the spaces necessary for the remaking of a democratic community. For this to happen, there must of course be a new commitment to intelligence, a new fidelity in communication, a new regard for imagination. It would mean fresh and sometimes startling winds blowing through the classrooms of the nation. It would mean the granting of audibility to numerous voices seldom heard before and, at once, an involvement with all sorts of young people being provoked to make their own the multilinguality needed for structuring of contemporary experience and thematizing lived worlds. The languages required include many of the traditional modes of sense-making: the academic disciplines, the fields of study. But none of them must ever be thought of as complete or all-encompassing, developed as they have been to respond to particular kinds of questions posed at particular moments in time. Turned, as lenses or perspectives, on the shared world of actualities, they cannot but continue resonating and reforming in the light of new undercurrents, new questions, new uncertainties.

Let us say young high school students are studying history. Clearly, they require some understanding of the rules of evidence where the historical record is concerned. They need to distinguish among sources, to single out among multiple determinants those forces that can be identified as causal, to find the places where chance cuts across necessity, to recognize when calculations are appropriate and when they are not. All this takes reflective comprehension of the norms governing the discipline of history. But this does not end or exhaust such study. There is a consciousness now, as there was not in time past, of the significance of doing history "from the ground up," of penetrating the so-called "cultures of silence" in order to discover what ordinary farmers and storekeepers and elementary schoolteachers and street children and Asian newcomers think and have thought about an event like the Holocaust or the Vietnam War or the bombing of Hiroshima or the repression in South Africa that continues to affect them directly or indirectly even as it recedes into the visualizable past. They need to be empowered to reflect on and talk about what happened in its varying connections with other events in the present as well as the past. And they may be brought to find out that a range of informed viewpoints may be just as important when it comes to understanding the Civil War, or the industrial revolution, or the slave trade, or the Children's Crusade. Clearly, if the voices of participants or near-participants (front-line soldiers, factory workers, slaves, crusaders) could be heard, whole dimensions of new understanding (and perplexity and uncertainty) would be disclosed. The same is true with respect to demographic studies, studies based on census rolls or tax collections, studies that include diaries and newspaper stories and old photographs. Turning the tools and techniques of history to resources of this kind often means opening up new spaces for study, metaphorical spaces sometimes, places for "speculative audacity." Such efforts may provide experiences of freedom in the study of history, because they unleash imagination in unexpected ways. They draw the mind to what lies beyond the accustomed boundaries and often to what is not yet. They do so as persons become more and more aware of the unanswered questions, the unexplored corners, the nameless faces behind the forgotten windows. These are the obstacles to be transcended if understanding is to be gained. And it is in the transcending, as we have seen, that freedom is often achieved.

The same can be said for the other disciplines and fields of study in the social and natural sciences; and, even among the exact sciences, a heightened curiosity may accompany the growth of feelings of connection between human hands and minds and the objects of study, whether they are rocks or stars or memory cores. Again, it is a matter of questioning and sense-making from a grounded vantage point, an interpretive vantage point, in a way that eventually sheds some light on the commonsense world, in a way that is always perspectival and therefore forever incomplete. The most potent metaphor for this can be found at the end of Melville's chapter called "Cetology" in the novel *Moby Dick*. The chapter deals with the essentially futile effort to provide a "systematized exhibition of the whale in his broad genera," or to classify the constituents of a chaos. And finally:

> It was stated at the outset, that this system would not be here, and at once, perfected. You cannot but plainly see that I have kept my word. But now I leave my cetological System standing thus unfinished, even as the great Cathedral of Cologne was left, with the crane still standing upon the top of the uncompleted tower. For small erections may be finished by their first architects; grand ones, true ones, ever leave the copestone to posterity. God keep me from ever completing anything. This whole book is but a draught—nay, but the draught of a draught. Oh, Time, Strength, Cash, and patience! (1851/1981, p. 148)

To recognize the role of perspective and vantage point, to recognize at the same time that there are always multiple perspectives and multiple vantage points, is to recognize that no accounting, disciplinary or otherwise, can ever be finished or complete. There is always more. There is always possibility. And this is where the space opens for the pursuit of freedom. Much the same can be said about experiences with art objects—not only literary texts, but music, painting, dance. They have the capacity, when authentically attended to, to enable persons to hear and to see what they would not ordinarily hear and see, to offer visions of consonance and dissonance that are unfamiliar and indeed abnormal, to disclose the incomplete profiles of the world. As importantly, in this context, they have the capacity to defamiliarize experience: to begin with the overly familiar and transfigure it into something different enough to make those who are awakened hear and see.

Generalizations with regard to what forms possess such potential for different people are tempting, but they must be set aside. Jazz and the blues have long had a transformative, often liberating effect on many populations, for example. We have only to read the musical history of our country, recall the stories of our great black musicians, heed such novels as *Invisible Man* (constructed, its author said, according to the patterns of the blues), take note of the importance of jazz in European art forms throughout the century, see how the Jazz Section of the Czech dissident movement has become the live center of dissent. The ways in which the blues have given rise to rock music and what are called "raps" testify as well to a power, not merely to embody and express the suffering of oppressed and constricted lives, but to name them somehow, to identify the gaps between what is and what is longed for, what (if the sphere of freedom is ever developed) will some day come to be.

Recent discoveries of women's novels, like discoveries of black literature, have certainly affected the vision of those reared in the traditions of so-called "great" literature, as they have the constricted visions of those still confined by outmoded ideas of gender. The growing ability to look at even classical works through new critical lenses has enabled numerous readers, of both genders, to apprehend previously unknown renderings of their lived worlds. Not only have many begun coming to literature with the intent of *achieving* it as meaningful through realization by means of perspectival readings. Many have begun engaging in what Mikhail Bakhtin called "dialogism," viewing literary texts as spaces where multiple voices and multiple discourses intersect and interact (1981, pp. 259–422). Even to confront what Bakhtin calls "heteroglossia" in a novel is to enlarge one's experience with multiplicity of perspectives and, at once, with the spheres that can open in the midst of pluralities.

With *Invisible Man* in mind, we might recall the point that invisibility represents a condition in the mind of the one who encounters the black person and draw implications for the ways we have looked at other strangers, and even for the ways we have looked at those posited as "other" or as enemies. We can find ourselves reading so-

called canonical works like *Jane Eyre* and become astonished by a
newly grasped interpretation of the "madwoman" imprisoned up-
stairs in Mr. Rochester's house. Shocked into a new kind of awareness, we find ourselves pushing back the boundaries again, hearing
new voices, exploring new discourses, unearthing new possibilities.
We can ponder such works as Tillie Olsen's "I Stand There Ironing"
or "Tell Me a Riddle" and uncover dimensions of oppression, dream,
and possibility never suspected before. We can look again at Gabriel
García Márquez's *One Hundred Years of Solitude* and find ourselves
opening windows in our experience to startling renderings of time,
death, and history that subvert more of our certainties. It is not only,
however, in the domains of the hitherto "silent" cultures that transformations of our experience can take place. There is a sense in
which the history of any art form carries with it a history of occasions for new visions, new modes of defamiliarization, at least in
cases where artists thrust away the auras, and broke in some way
with the past.

It has been clear in music, pushing back the horizons of silence
for at least a century, opening new frequencies for ears willing to
risk new sounds. It has been true of dance, as pioneers of movement
and visual metaphor uncover new possibilities in the human body
and therefore for embodied consciousnesses in the world. In painting, it has been dramatically the case. An example can be found in the
work of the painter John Constable, who abandoned old paradigms
of studio painting and studio light and began sketching his subjects
in the open air. Breaking through "horizons of expectation," as the
critic Ernst Gombrich writes (1965, p. 34), Constable enabled specta-
tors to perceive green in the landscape, rather than rendering it in
the traditional manner in gradations of brown. He defamiliarized the
visible world, in effect, making accessible shadings and nuances
never suspected before. We can say similar things about numerous
visual artists, if we are enabled, say, to see them against their
forerunners; moving through the "museums without walls," listen-
ing to those Merleau-Ponty called the "voices of silence," we can
discover ourselves variously on an always-changing place on earth.
Giotto, della Francesca, Botticelli, Michelangelo, Raphael, Poussin:
The names sound, the doors open to vista after vista. Exemplary for
moderns may be Claude Monet making visible the modelling effects
of light on objects once seen as solidly and objectively *there*. Some can
recall the multiple studies of haystacks in his garden at different
seasons of the year or of Rouen Cathedral at different times of day.
Recalling, we are reminded again how visions of fixity can be trans-

formed, how time itself can take on new meanings for the perceiver, for the one choosing to journey through works of visual art. And we can (we ought to) recall Pablo Picasso's abrupt expansion of Western observers' conceptions of humanity and space with his "Demoiselles d'Avignon" and its African and Iberian visages, or his imaging of unendurable pain in the "Guernica."

Of course, such visions are unknown in most of our classrooms; and relatively few people are informed enough or even courageous enough actually to "see." And it must be acknowledged that, for all their emancipatory potential, the arts cannot be counted on to liberate, to ensure an education for freedom. Nonetheless, for those authentically concerned about the "birth of meaning," about breaking through the surfaces, about teaching others to "read" their own worlds, art forms must be conceived of as ever-present possibility. They ought not to be treated as decorative, as frivolous. They ought to be, if transformative teaching is our concern, a central part of curriculum, wherever it is devised. How can it be irrelevant, for example, to include such images as those of William Blake, with contraries and paradoxes that make it forever impossible to place the "lamb" and the "tiger" in distinctive universes, to separate the "marriage" from the "hearse"? How can it be of only extracurricular interest to turn to Emily Dickinson, for instance, and find normal views of experience disrupted and transformed? She wrote:

> I stepped from plank to plank
>   So slow and cautiously;
> The stars about my head I felt,
>   About my feet the sea.
> I knew not but the next
>   Would be my final inch,—
> This gave me that precarious gait
>   Some call experience.
>   (1890/1959, p. 166)

The spaces widen in the poem—from plank to plank under an open sky. She identifies experience itself with a "precarious gait"; and the risk involved is emphasized. Reading such a work, we cannot but find our own world somehow defamiliarized. Defamiliarized, it discloses aspects of experience ordinarily never seen. Critical awareness may be somehow enhanced, as new possibilities open for reflection. Poetry does not offer us empirical or documentary truth, but it enables us to "know" in unique ways. So many poems come to mind, among them W. H. Auden's "Surgical Ward," which may emerge from memory because of the AIDS epidemic, or because of a concern about distancing and lack of care. He wrote of the remoteness of those who "are and suffer; that is all they do" and of the isolation of the sufferers compared with those who believe "in the common world of the uninjured and cannot imagine isolation—" (1970, pp. 44-45). Any one of a hundred others might have come to mind: the choice is arbitrary. A writer, like the writer of this book, can only hope to activate the memories of *her* readers, to awaken, to strike sparks.

The same is true, even more true, when it comes to novels and plays: The occasions for revelation and disclosure are beyond counting. In my train of thought (and readers will locate themselves in their own), I find Antigone, committed to her sense of what is moral and dying for her cause; King Lear, with all artifice and "superfluity" abandoned on the heath in the raging storm. I somehow see Lucifer falling in *Paradise Lost* and continually falling, reappearing at the end of James Joyce's *A Portrait of the Artist as a Young Man* when Stephen Dedalus says, "I will not serve." And then, remembering Joyce, I hear that resounding "Yes" at the end of Molly Bloom's soliloquy in *Ulysses*. In the background, softly, stubbornly, there is Bartleby's "I prefer not to" in the Melville story; there is the dying Ivan Ilyitch in the Tolstoy story, speaking of himself as "little Vanya" to the peasant holding his legs; there is the shadow of the little girl who hung herself in Dostoevsky's *The Possessed*. There are the soldiers described in Malraux's *Man's Fate*, young soldiers about to be executed on the Lithuanian front and forced to take off their trousers in the snow. They begin to sneeze, "and those sneezes were so intensely human in that dawn of execution, that the machine-gunners, instead of firing, waited—waited for life to become less indiscreet" (1936, p. 76). Indiscreet—and I see the house beaten by the storms and the dilapidations of time in the "Time Passes" section of Virginia Woolf's *To the Lighthouse*; Willa Cather's Paul (in "Paul's Case") and the winter roses and a boy's death on the railroad tracks. There are the spare, lace-curtained bedrooms and the slave women in red in Margaret Atwood's *The Handmaid's Tale*; and, in another future, there is the stark transcendence of the rocket in *Gravity's Rainbow* by Thomas Pynchon. There is Mark Helprin's white horse in the snow-bound city in *Winter's Tale*, the "air-borne toxic event" in Don DeLillo's *White Noise*.

Any reader might go on to recall how, as Herbert Marcuse has put it, "art is committed to that perception of the world which alienates individuals from their functional existence and performance in society" (1978, p. 9). An education for freedom must move beyond function, beyond the subordination of persons to external ends. It must move beyond mere performance to action, which entails the taking of initiatives. This is not meant to imply that aesthetic engagements, because they take place in domains of freedom, separate or alienate learners so fully from the tasks of the world that they become incapacitated for belonging or for membership or for work itself. Marcuse also spoke of an aesthetic transformation as a "vehicle of recognition," drawing the perceiver away from "the mystifying power of the given" (1978, p. 72). He was pointing to an emancipatory possibility of relevance for an education in and for freedom. Encounters with the arts alone will not realize it; but the arts will help open the situations that require interpretation, will help disrupt the walls that obscure the spaces, the spheres of freedom to which educators might some day attend.

With situations opening, students may become empowered to engage in some sort of *praxis*, engaged enough to name the obstacles in the way of their shared becoming. They may at first be identified with the school itself, with the neighborhood, with the family, with fellow-beings in the endangered world. They may be identified with prejudices, rigidities, suppressed violence: All these can petrify or impinge on the sphere of freedom. As Foucault would have it, persons may be made into subjects, docile bodies to be "subjected, used, transformed, and improved" (1977, p. 136). It is not merely the structures of class, race, and gender relations that embody such power and make it felt in classrooms. Much the same can happen through the differential distribution of knowledge, through a breaking of what is distributed into discrete particles, through an unwarranted classification of a "chaos."

Having attended to women's lives and the lives of many strangers, we are aware of the relation between the subjugation of voices and the silencing of memories. All these have often been due to the insidious workings of power or the maintenance of what has been called "hegemony" (Entwhistle, 1979, pp. 12–14). Hegemony, as explained by the Italian philosopher Antonio Gramsci, means direction by moral and intellectual persuasion, not by physical coercion. That is what makes it a matter of such concern for those interested in education for freedom. The persuasion is often so quiet, so seductive, so disguised that it renders young people acquiescent to power without their realizing it. The persuasion becomes most effective when the method used obscures what is happening in the learners' minds. Strangely, the acquiescence, the acceptance, may find expression through dropping out or other modes of alienation, as much as through a bland compliance to what is taken to be the given. This may be because the message or the direction emphasizes an opportunity system or a stratification system offering a limited range of possibilities, apparently attentive to but a few modes of being. This becomes most drastically clear in the case of youngsters whose IQs, according to current testing practices, are low. Ours is not a society that ponders fulfilling options for people with low IQs. Lacking an awareness of alternatives, lacking a vision of realizable possibilities, the young (left unaware of the messages they are given) have no hope of achieving freedom.

In the classroom opened to possibility and at once concerned with inquiry, critiques must be developed that uncover what masquerade as neutral frameworks, or what Rorty calls "a set of rules which will tell us how rational agreement can be reached on what would settle the issue on every point where statements seem to conflict" (1979, p. 315). Teachers, like their students, have to learn to love the questions, as they come to realize that there can be no final agreements or answers, no final commensurability. And we have been talking about stories that open perspectives on communities grounded in trust, flowering by means of dialogue, kept alive in open spaces where freedom can find a place.

Looking back, we can discern individuals in their we-relations with others, inserting themselves in the world by means of projects, embarking on new beginnings in spaces they open themselves. We can recall them—Thomas Jefferson, the Grimké sisters, Susan B. Anthony, Jane Addams, Frederick Douglass, W. E. B. DuBois, Martin Luther King, John Dewey, Carol Gilligan, Nel Noddings, Mary Daly—opening public spaces where freedom is the mainspring, where people create themselves by acting in concert. For Hannah Arendt, "power corresponds to the human ability . . . to act in concert. Power is never the property of an individual; it belongs to a group and remains in existence only so long as the group keeps together" (1972, p. 143). Power may be thought of, then, as "empowerment," a condition of possibility for human and political life and, yes, for education as well. But spaces have to be opened in the schools and around the schools; the windows have to let in the fresh air. The poet Mark Strand writes:

> It is all in the mind, you say, and has
> nothing to do with happiness. The coming of cold,
> The coming of heat, the mind has all the time in the world.
> You take my arm and say something will happen,

something unusual for which we were always prepared,
like the sun arriving after a day in Asia,
like the moon departing after a night with us.

(1984, p. 126)

And Adrienne Rich, calling a poem "Integrity" and beginning, "A wild patience has taken me this far" (1981, p. 8). There is a need for a wild patience. And, when freedom is the question, it is always a time to begin.

References

Addams, J. 1899. "A Function of the Social Settlement." In *Jane Addams on Education*, ed. E. C. Lagemann, pp. 74–97. New York: Teachers College Press, 1985.
———. 1902. *Democracy and Social Ethics*. New York: The Macmillan Co.
———. 1910. *Twenty Years at Hull-House*. New York: The Macmillan Co.
Arendt, H. 1958. *The Human Condition*. Chicago: University of Chicago Press.
———. 1961a. *Between Past and Present*. New York: The Viking Press.
———. 1961b. *Men in Dark Times*. New York: The Viking Press.
———. 1968. *On Revolution*. New York: Harvest Books.
———. 1972. *Crises of the Republic*. New York: Harcourt Brace Jovanovich.
Aristotle. *Nichomachean Ethics*, Book VIII. Trans. W. D. Ross. In *Introduction to Aristotle*, ed. R. McKeon. New York: The Modern Library, 1972.
Auden, W. H. 1970. *Selected Poetry of W. H. Auden*. New York: Vintage Books.
Atwood, M. 1986. *The Handmaid's Tale*. New York: Houghton Mifflin Co.
Bakhtin, M. M. 1981. *The Dialogic Imagination*. Austin: University of Texas Press.
Belenky, M. F., et al. 1986. *Women's Ways of Knowing*. New York: Basic Books.
Bellah, R. N., et al. 1985. *Habits of the Heart*. Berkeley: University of California Press.
Bellow, S. 1953. *The Adventures of Augie March*. New York: The Viking Press.
———. 1969. *Dangling Man*. New York: Meridian Fiction.
Berlin, I. 1970. *Four Essays on Liberty*. New York: Oxford University Press.
Brown, S. A. 1971. "Strong Men." In *The Black Poets*, ed. D. Randall, pp. 113–115. New York: Bantam Books.
Callahan, R. E. 1962. *Education and the Cult of Efficiency*. Chicago: University of Chicago Press, 1964.
Chodorow, N. 1978. *The Reproduction of Mothering: Psychoanalysis and Sociology of Gender*. Berkeley: University of California Press.
Chopin, K. 1899. *The Awakening*. New York: Avon Books, 1972.
Coles, R. 1967. *Children of Crisis*. Boston: Atlantic-Little Brown & Co.
Cott, N. F., ed. 1972. *Root of Bitterness*. New York: E. P. Dutton & Co.

Covello, L. 1958. *The Heart Is the Teacher*. New York: McGraw-Hill.

Crane, S. 1892. *Maggie: A Girl of the Streets*. New York: Fawcett World Library, 1960.

Cremin, L. A. 1961. *The Transformation of the School: Progressivism in American Education, 1876–1957*. New York: Alfred A. Knopf.

Daly, M. 1978. *Gyn/Ecology: The Metaethics of Radical Feminism*. Boston: Beacon Press.

Davis, A. F. 1973. *American Heroine: The Life and Legend of Jane Addams*. New York: Oxford University Press.

DeLillo, D. 1985. *White Noise*. Viking Penguin Press.

De Tocqueville, A. 1840. *Democracy in America*, Volume II. Ed. P. Bradley. New York: Vintage Books. 1954.

Dewey, J. 1902. *The Child and the Curriculum*. In *Dewey on Education*, ed. M. Dworkin. New York: Teachers College Press, 1959.

———. 1916. *Democracy and Education*. New York: Macmillan Co.

———. 1927. *The Public and Its Problems*. Athens, OH: Swallow Press, 1954.

———. 1928. "Philosophies of Freedom." In his *On Experience, Nature, and Freedom*, ed. R. Bernstein. New York: The Liberal Arts Press, 1960.

———. 1931. *Philosophy and Civilization*. New York: Minton, Balch & Co.

———. 1934. *Art as Experience*. New York: Minton, Balch & Co.

———. 1937. "Democracy and Educational Administration." In *Education Today*. New York: G. P. Putnam's Sons, 1940.

———. 1938. *Experience and Education*. New York: Collier Books, 1963.

———. 1939. *Freedom and Culture*. New York: Capricorn Books, 1963.

———. 1940. "Presenting Thomas Jefferson." In *The Living Thoughts of Thomas Jefferson*, ed. J. Dewey. Philadelphia: David McKay Co.

Dickinson, E. 1890. *Selected Poems & Letters of Emily Dickinson*. Ed. R. N. Linscott. Garden City, NY: Doubleday Anchor Books, 1959.

Didion, J. 1970. *Play It as It Lays*. New York: Farrar, Straus, & Giroux.

Di Donato, P. 1939. *Christ in Concrete*. New York: Bobbs Merrill Co.

Dos Passos, J. 1937. *The 42nd Parallel*. New York: Modern Library.

Dostoevsky, F. 1864. *Notes from Underground*. Trans. Constance Garnett. In *The Short Novels of Dostoevsky*. New York: Dial Press. 1945.

———. 1879–1880. *The Brothers Karamazov*. Trans. Constance Garnett. New York: Modern Library, 1945.

Douglas, A. 1977. *The Feminization of American Culture*. New York: Alfred A. Knopf.

Douglass, F. 1855. *My Bondage and My Freedom*. Boston: DeWolfe, Fiske, & Co.

———. 1857. "Two Speeches." In *Eyewitness*, ed. W. L. Katz. New York: Pitman Publishing Co., 1967.

DuBois, W. E. B. 1903. *The Souls of Black Folk*. New York: New American Library, 1982.

———. 1972. *W. E. B. DuBois: A Reader*. Ed. M. Weinberg. New York: Harper Torchbooks.

Eagleton, T. 1983. *Literary Theory: An Introduction.* Minneapolis: University of Minnesota Press.

Eliot, T. S. 1958. *The Complete Poems and Plays, 1909-1950.* New York: Harcourt, Brace & Co.

Ellison, R. 1952. *Invisible Man.* New York: New American Library.

Emerson, R. W. 1837. "The American Scholar." In *Emerson on Education,* ed. H. M. Jones, pp. 71-101. New York: Teachers College Press, 1966.

———. 1841. "Self-Reliance." In *Emerson on Education,* ed. H. M. Jones, pp. 102-132. New York: Teachers College Press, 1966.

Entwhistle, H. 1979. *Antonio Gramsci.* London: Routledge & Kegan Paul.

Fante, J. 1966. "The Odyssey of a Wop." In *Children of the Uprooted,* ed. O. Handlin, pp. 387-401. New York: George Braziller.

Farrell, J. T. 1934. *The Young Manhood of Studs Lonigan.* New York: The World Publishing Company, 1944.

Faulkner, W. 1942. *The Bear.* In *Three Famous Short Novels.* New York: Vintage Books, 1958.

———. 1946. *The Sound and the Fury.* New York: Modern Library.

Fetterley, J., ed. 1985. *Provisions: A Reader from 19th Century Women.* Bloomington: Indiana University Press.

Fitzgerald, F. S. 1926. *The Great Gatsby.* New York: Charles Scribner's Sons, 1953.

Flexner, E. 1975. *Centuries of Struggle: The Women's Rights Movement in the United States.* Cambridge, MA: Harvard University Press.

Flynn, E. G. 1955. *I Speak My Own Piece.* New York: Masses and Mainstream.

Foucault, M. 1977a. *Language, Counter-Memory, Practice.* Ed. D. F. Bouchard. Ithaca: Cornell University Press.

———. 1977b. *Power/Knowledge: Selected Interviews and Other Writings.* Ed. C. Gordon. New York: Pantheon Books.

———. 1982. "The Subject and Power." In *Michel Foucault: Beyond Structuralism and Hermeneutics.* Chicago: The University of Chicago Press.

———. 1984. *The Foucault Reader.* Ed. P. Rabinow. New York: Pantheon Books.

Freire, P. 1970. *Pedagogy of the Oppressed.* New York: Herder and Herder.

Fromm, E. 1941. *Escape from Freedom.* New York: Farrar & Rinehart.

Gadamer, H-G. 1975. "Hermeneutics and Social Science." *Cultural Hermeneutics, 2.*

———. 1977. *Philosophical Hermeneutics.* Ed. D. E. Linge, pp. 307-316. Berkeley: University of California Press.

García Márquez, G. J. 1967. *One Hundred Years of Solitude.* Trans. G. Rabasso. New York: Harper & Row, 1970.

Geertz, C. 1983. *Local Knowledge.* New York: Basic Books.

Giddings, P. 1984. *Where and When I Enter: The Impact of Black Women on Race and Sex in America.* New York: William Morrow and Co.

Gilligan, C. 1982. *In a Different Voice.* Cambridge: Harvard University Press.

Glazer, N., & Moynihan, D. P. 1964. *Beyond the Melting Pot,* 2d edition. Cambridge: M.I.T. Press, 1973.

Gombrich, E. 1965. *Art and Illusion*. New York: Pantheon Press.

Gould, C. C. 1976. "The Woman Question: Philosophy of Liberation and the Liberation of Philosophy." In *Women and Philosophy*, ed. C. C. Gould & M. W. Wartofsky, pp. 5–44. New York: Capricorn Books.

Grimké, S. 1838. "Letters on the Equality of the Sexes." In *Root of Bitterness*, ed. N. Cott. New York: E. P. Dutton, 1972.

Habermas, J. 1971. *Knowledge and Human Interests*. Boston: Beacon Press.

Hampshire. S. 1975. *Freedom of the Individual*. Princeton: Princeton University Press.

Handlin, O., ed. 1966. *Children of the Uprooted*. New York: George Braziller.

Hare, R. M. 1965. *Freedom and Reason*. New York: Oxford University Press.

Harris, W. T. 1900. "Elementary Education." In *Monographs on Education in the United States*, ed. N. M. Butler. Albany, NY: J. B. Lyon.

Hawthorne, N. 1850. *The Scarlet Letter and Selected Tales*. New York: Penguin Books, 1969.

Hayden, T. 1967. "Student Social Action." In *The New Student Left*, ed. M. Cohen & D. Hale, pp. 272–289. Boston: Beacon Press.

Heidegger, M. 1971. *Poetry, Language, and Thought*. Trans. A. Hofstadter. New York: Harper & Row.

Helprin, M. 1983. *Winter's Tale*. New York: Pocket Books.

Hemingway, E. 1929. *A Farewell to Arms*. London: Jonathan Cape, 1952.

Henry, J. 1963. *Culture Against Man*. New York: Random House.

Hoffman, N. 1981. *Woman's "True" Profession: Voices from the History of Teaching*. Old Westbury, NY: The Feminist Press.

Howe, I. 1976. *World of Our Fathers*. New York: Harcourt Brace Jovanovich.

Hughes, L. 1968. "As I Grew Older." In *Black Voices*, ed. A. Chapman, p. 426. New York: New American Library.

Ignatieff, M. 1984. *The Needs of Strangers*. London: Chatto & Windus.

James, H. 1881. *The Portrait of a Lady*. New York: New American Library, 1979.

James, W. 1900. *Talks to Teachers on Psychology: And to Students on Some of Life's Ideals*. New York: Henry Holt and Company, 1906.

Jefferson, T. 1776. "The Declaration of Independence as Adopted by Congress, July 4, 1776." In *Crusade Against Ignorance*, ed. G. C. Lee, pp. 28–32. New York: Teachers College Press, 1972.

———. 1779. "A Bill for the More General Diffusion of Knowledge." In *Crusade Against Ignorance*, ed. G. C. Lee, pp. 83–91. New York: Teachers College Press, 1972.

———. 1800. "Letter to Dr. Benjamin Rush." In *Papers of Thomas Jefferson*, Vol. 2, ed. Julian P. Boyd. Princeton: Princeton University Press, 1950.

———. 1801. "First Inaugural Address." In *Crusade Against Ignorance*, ed. G. C. Lee, pp. 50–54. New York: Teachers College Press, 1972.

Joyce, J. 1916. *A Portrait of the Artist as a Young Man*. New York: Viking Press, 1955.

Kallen, H. 1915, February 18. "Democracy vs. The Melting Pot." *The Nation*.

Kant, I. 1797. *The Doctrine of Virtue.* Part II of *The Metaphysics of Morals.* Trans. Mary J. Gregor. New York: Harper Torchbooks, 1964.

Kazin, A. 1979. *New York Jew.* New York: Vintage Books.

Keller, E. F. 1985. *Reflections on Gender and Science.* New Haven: Yale University Press.

Kelley, M. 1984. *Private Woman, Public Stage: Literary Domesticity in Nineteenth Century America.* New York: Oxford University Press.

King, M. L. 1964. *Why We Can't Wait.* New York: Harper & Row.

Kohlberg, L. 1971. "Stages of Moral Development as a Basis for Moral Education." In *Moral Education: Interdisciplinary Approaches,* ed. C. M. Beck, B. S. Crittenden, & E. V. Sullivan. New York: Newman Press.

Konrad, G. 1974. *The Caseworker.* New York: Harcourt Brace Jovanovich.

Kristeva, J. 1975. "The System and the Speaking Subject." In *The Tell-Tale Sign: A Survey of Semiotics,* ed. T. A. Sebeok. Lisse, Netherlands: Peter de Ridder Press.

Kundera, M. 1984. *The Unbearable Lightness of Being.* New York: Harper & Row.

Lagemann, E. C. 1979. *A Generation of Women: Education in the Lives of Progressive Reformers.* New York: Harvard University Press.

Lasch, C. 1984. *The Minimal Self.* New York: W. W. Norton & Co.

MacKinnon, C. A. 1981. "Feminism, Marxism, Method, and the State: An Agenda for Theory." In *Feminist Theory: A Critique of Ideology,* ed. N. O. Keohane, M. Z. Rosaldo, & B. C. Gelpi. Chicago: University of Chicago Press.

Mailer, N. 1968. *The Armies of the Night.* New York: New American Library.

Malamud, B. 1957. *The Assistant.* New York: New American Library.

Malraux, A. 1936. *Man's Fate.* New York: Modern Library.

Mann, H. 1838. "The Necessity of Education in a Republican Government." In *Ideology and Power in the Age of Jackson,* ed. E. C. Rozwenc, pp. 143–161. Garden City, NY: Doubleday Anchor Books, 1964.

———. 1837–1848. *The Republic and the School: Horace Mann on the Education of Free Men,* ed. L. A. Cremin. New York: Teachers College Press, 1957.

Marcuse, H. 1978. *The Aesthetic Dimension.* Boston: Beacon Press.

McDermott, A. 1987. *That Night.* New York: Farrar, Straus, & Giroux.

McPherson, J. M. 1968. "The Anti-Slavery Legacy." In *Towards a New Past: Dissenting Essays in American History,* ed. B. J. Bernstein, pp. 126–157. New York: Pantheon Books.

Melville, H. 1851. *Moby Dick.* Berkeley: University of California Press, 1981.

———. 1856. "Benito Cereno." In *Selected Writings: Complete Short Stories.* New York: Modern Library, 1952.

———. 1949. "The Tartarus of Maids." In *Selected Writings: Complete Short Stories.* New York: Modern Library, 1952.

Merleau-Ponty, M. 1962. *Phenomenology of Perception.* New York: Humanities Press, 1967.

———. 1964. *The Primacy of Perception.* Evanston, IL: Northwestern University Press.

———. 1967. *The Structure of Behavior*. Boston: Beacon Press.

———. 1968. *The Visible and the Invisible*. Evanston: Northwestern University Press.

Miller, S. 1986. *The Good Mother*. New York: Harper & Row.

Miller, W. L. 1975. *Of Thee, Nevertheless, I Sing*. New York: Harcourt Brace Jovanovich.

Morrison, T. 1975. *Sula*. New York: Bantam Books.

Myrdal, G. 1962. *An American Dilemma*. New York: Harper & Row.

Nizan, P. 1973. *Antoine Bloyé*. Trans. Edmund Stevens. New York: Monthly Review Press.

Noddings, N. 1984. *Caring: A Feminine Approach to Ethics and Moral Education*. Berkeley: University of California Press.

Oliver, D. W., & Bane, M. J. 1971. "Moral Education: Is Reasoning Enough?" In *Moral Education: Interdisciplinary Approaches*, ed. C. M. Beck, B. S. Crittenden, & E. V. Sullivan. New York: Newman Press.

Olsen, T. 1978. *Silences*. New York: Delacorte Press.

Passmore, J. 1975. "On Teaching to Be Critical." In *Education and Reason*, ed. R. F. Dearden, P. H. Hirst, & R. S. Peters, pp. 415–433. London: Routledge & Kegan Paul.

Percy, W. 1979. *The Moviegoer*. New York: Alfred A. Knopf.

Peters, R. S. 1970. "Concrete Principles and the Rational Passions." In *Moral Education*, ed. N. F. Sizer & T. R. Sizer. Cambridge: Harvard University Press.

———. 1975. "Education and Human Development." In *Education and Reason*, ed. R. F. Dearden, P. H. Hirst, & R. S. Peters, pp. 501–520. London: Routledge & Kegan Paul.

Piaget, J. 1977. *The Essential Piaget*. Ed. H. E. Gruber & J. J. Voneche. New York: Basic Books.

Polanyi, M. 1964. "The Logic of Tacit Inference." In *Knowing and Being*, ed. M. Greene. Chicago: University of Chicago Press, 1969.

Pynchon, T. 1973. *Gravity's Rainbow*. New York: Viking Press.

Raskin, M. 1971. *Being and Doing*. New York: Random House.

Reich, R. B. 1986. *Tales of a New America*. New York: Times Books.

Rich, A. 1981. *A Wild Patience Has Taken Me This Far*. New York: W. W. Norton.

Ricoeur, P. 1966. *Freedom and Nature*. Evanston: Northwestern University Press.

———. 1983. *Hermeneutics and the Human Sciences*. Ed. J. B. Thompson. Cambridge: Cambridge University Press.

Rodriguez, R. 1983. *Hunger of Memory*. New York: Bantam Books.

Rorty, R. 1979. *Philosphy and the Mirror of Nature*. Princeton: Princeton University Press.

———. 1985. "Solidarity or Objectivity?" In *Post-Analytic Philosophy*, ed. J. Rajchman & C. West. New York: Columbia University Press.

Rose, W. L. 1982. *Slavery and Freedom*. New York: Oxford University Press.

Ross, S. D. 1973. *The Nature of Moral Responsibility*. Detroit: Wayne State University Press.

Rukeyser, M. 1962. "Käthe Kollwitz." In *by a Woman writt*, ed. Joan Goulianos, pp. 373–378. New York: The Bobbs-Merrill Co., 1973.

Sartre, J-P. 1948. *Anti-Semite and Jew*. New York: Schocken Books.

———. 1956. *Being and Nothingness*. New York: Philosophical Library.

———. 1963. *Search for a Method*. New York: Alfred A. Knopf.

Schaar, J. J. 1979, May. "Melville's *Benito Cereno*." *Theory and Society*, 7, 417–452.

Schneir, M., ed. 1972. *Feminism: The Essential Historical Writings*. New York: Vintage Books.

Schon, D. A. 1983. *The Reflective Practitioner*. New York: Basic Books.

Sennett, R. 1979. *The Fall of Public Man*. New York: Alfred A. Knopf.

Skvorecky, J. 1984. *The Engineer of Human Souls*. New York: Alfred A. Knopf.

Smith, H. N. 1950. *Virgin Land: The American West as Symbol and Myth*. New York: Vintage Books, 1959.

Steinbeck, J. 1939. *The Grapes of Wrath*. New York: Viking Press.

Strand, M. 1939. "So You Say." In *Selected Poems*. New York: Viking Press.

Summer, William Graham. 1906. *Folkways*. Boston: Ginn & Co.

Swados, H., ed. 1966. *The American Writer and the Great Depression*. Indianapolis: Bobbs-Merrill Company.

Taylor, C. 1977. "Interpretation and the Sciences of Man." In *Understanding and Social Inquiry*, ed. F. R. Dallmayr & T. A. McCarthy, pp. 101–131. Notre Dame: Notre Dame University Press.

———. 1985. *Hegel and Modern Society*. Cambridge: Cambridge University Press.

Thernstrom, S. 1968. "Urbanization, Migration, and Social Mobility in Late Nineteenth-century America." In *Towards a New Past: Dissenting Essays in American History*, ed. B. J. Bernstein, pp. 158–175. New York: Pantheon Books.

Thoreau, H. D. 1854. *Walden*. New York: Washington Square Press, 1963.

———. 1863. "Life Without Principle." In *The American Transcendentalists*, ed. P. Miller. Garden City, NY: Doubleday Anchor Books, 1957.

Twain, M. 1885. *The Adventures of Huckleberry Finn*. New York: New American Library, 1959.

Tyack, D. B. 1974. *The One Best System: A History of American Urban Education*. Cambridge: Harvard University Press.

Tyack, D. B., & Hansot, E. 1982. *Managers of Virtue: Public School Leadership in America, 1820–1980*. New York: Harper Colophon Books.

Tyler, A. F. 1944. *Freedom's Ferment*. New York: Harper Torchbooks, 1962.

Unger, R. M. 1975. *Knowledge and Politics*. New York: Free Press.

Walker, A. 1976. *Meridian*. New York: Washington Square Press.

———. 1982. *The Color Purple*. New York: Washington Square Press.

Wertheimer, B. M. 1977. *We Were There: The Story of Working Women in America*. New York: Pantheon Books.

Wharton, E. 1905. *The House of Mirth*. New York: New American Library, 1964.

White, M. 1957. *Social Thought in America: The Revolt Against Formalism*. Boston: Beacon Press.

Whitman, W. 1855. *Leaves of Grass*. New York: Aventine Press, 1931.

Williams, J. 1987. *Eyes on the Prize: America's Civil Rights Years, 1954–1965*. New York: Viking Press.

Woolf, V. 1938. *To the Lighthouse*. London: J. M. Dent & Sons, 1962.

———. 1939. *Moments of Being*. New York: Harcourt Brace Jovanovich, 1976.

Wright, R. 1940. *Native Son*. New York: Harper & Brothers.

Yellin, J. F. 1981. "Written by Herself: Harriet Jacobs' Slave Narrative." *American Literature*, 53, 479–486.

Index

About the Author

Maxine Greene has been on the faculty of Teachers College, Columbia University, since 1965. Her courses have dealt with philosophy and history of education, social philosophy, aesthetic education, and literature. She has held the William F. Russell Chair in the Foundations of Education since 1975 and continues as professor of philosophy and education to work in interdisciplinary fields. Before coming to Teachers College, she taught at Montclair State College, New York University, and Brooklyn College of the City University of New York. She has lectured widely at universities and educational associations throughout the United States, is a past president of the Philosophy of Education Society and the American Educational Studies Association, and a past president of the American Educational Research Association. She has received numerous academic awards, including the Delta Gamma Kappa Award for the "Educational Book of the Year" for *Teacher as Stranger* in 1974 and two Phi Delta Kappa "Teacher of the Year" awards, and is the author of many journal articles and chapters in essay collections, as well as *Existential Encounters for Teachers, The Public School and the Private Vision*, and *Landscapes of Learning*. She holds honorary degrees from Lehigh University, Hofstra University, and Bank Street College of Education.